PRACTICE - ASSESS - DIAGNOSE

180 Days of
SOCIAL STUDIES
for First Grade

Author

Kathy Flynn, M.Ed.

SHELL EDUCATION

Publishing Credits

Corinne Burton, M.A.Ed., *Publisher*
Conni Medina, M.A.Ed., *Managing Editor*
Emily R. Smith, M.A.Ed., *Content Director*
Veronique Bos, *Creative Director*

Developed and Produced by
Focus Strategic Communications, Inc.

Project Manager: Adrianna Edwards
Editor: Cathy Fraccaro
Designer and Compositor: Ruth Dwight
Proofreader: Francine Geraci
Photo Researcher: Paula Joiner
Art: Deborah Crowle

Image Credits

Front cover (bottom left) Library of Congress [LC-DIG-ppmsca-19241]; p.37 Heidi Besen/Shutterstock; p.43 (middle) Aspen Photo/Shutterstock; p.43 (right) Herreid/iStock; p.55, p.56 NASA; p.55 Mario Breda/Shutterstock; p.58 Public Affairs Office/The United States Marine Corps; p.75 Rene Sturgell [CC BY-SA 3.0]; p.78 Records of the Office of the Chief Signal Officer; p.79 (bottom right) Gary J. Wood [CC BY-SA 2.0]; p.91 Lano Lan/Shutterstock; p.96 Library of Congress [LC-DIG-fsa-8a03228]; p.97 (left) Pictorial Press Ltd/Alamy; p.116 (center left) Library of Congress [LC-DIG-nclc-04337]; p.116 Sharon Day/Shutterstock; p.130 (bottom) Ollo/iStock; p.169 (top left) Grigorii Pisotsckii/Shutterstock; p.177 Denise Lett/Shutterstock; p.185 S-F/Shutterstock; all other images iStock and/or Shutterstock.

Standards

© 2014 Mid-continent Research for Education and Learning (McREL)
© 2010 National Council for the Social Studies (NCSS), The College, Career, and Civic Life (C3) Framework for Social Studies State Standards: Guidance for Enhancing the Rigor of K–12 Civics, Economics, Geography, and History

For information on how this resource meets national and other state standards, see pages 12–14. You may also review this information by visiting our website at www.teachercreatedmaterials.com/administrators/correlations/ and following the on-screen directions.

Shell Education

A division of Teacher Created Materials
5301 Oceanus Drive
Huntington Beach, CA 92649-1030
www.tcmpub.com/shell-education

ISBN 978-1-4258-1393-2

©2018 Shell Educational Publishing, Inc.

Table of Contents

Introduction 3

How to Use This Book 5

Standards Correlations 12

Daily Practice Pages 15

Answer Key 195

Rubric 204

Analysis Pages 205

Digital Resources 208

Introduction

In the complex global world of the 21st century, it is essential for citizens to have the foundational knowledge and analytic skills to understand the barrage of information surrounding them. An effective social studies program will provide students with these analytic skills and prepare them to understand and make intentional decisions about their country and the world. A well-designed social studies program develops active citizens who are able to consider multiple viewpoints and the possible consequences of various decisions.

The four strands of a social studies program enable students to understand their relationships with other people—those who are similar and those from diverse backgrounds. Students come to appreciate the foundations of the American democratic system and the importance of civic involvement. They have opportunities to understand the historic and economic forces that have resulted in the world and United States of today. They will also explore geography to better understand the nature of Earth and the effects of human interactions.

It is essential that the social studies program address more than basic knowledge. In each grade, content knowledge is a vehicle for students to engage in deep, rich thinking. They must problem solve, make decisions, work cooperatively as well as alone, make connections, and make reasoned value judgments. The world and the United States are rapidly changing. Students must be prepared for the world they will soon lead.

The Need for Practice

To be successful in today's social studies classrooms, students must understand both basic knowledge and the application of ideas to new or novel situations. They must be able to discuss and apply their ideas in coherent and rational ways. Practice is essential if they are to internalize social studies concepts, skills, and big ideas. Practice is crucial to help students have the experience and confidence to apply the critical-thinking skills needed to be active citizens in a global society.

Introduction *(cont.)*

Understanding Assessment

In addition to providing opportunities for frequent practice, teachers must be able to assess students' understanding of social studies concepts, big ideas, vocabulary, and reasoning. This is important so teachers can effectively address students' misconceptions and gaps, build on their current understanding, and challenge their thinking at an appropriate level. Assessment is a long-term process that involves careful analysis of student responses from a multitude of sources. In the social studies context, this could include classroom discussions, projects, presentations, practice sheets, or tests. When analyzing the data, it is important for teachers to reflect on how their teaching practices may have influenced students' responses and to identify those areas where additional instruction may be required. Essentially, the data gathered from assessment should be used to inform instruction: to slow down, to continue as planned, to speed up, or to reteach in a new way.

Best Practices for This Series

- Use the practice pages to introduce important social studies topics to your students.

- Use the Weekly Topics and Themes chart from pages 5–7 to align the content to what you're covering in class. Then, treat the pages in this book as jumping off points for that content.

- Use the practice pages as formative assessment of the key social studies disciplines: history, civics, geography, and economics.

- Use the weekly themes to engage students in content that is new to them.

- Encourage students to independently learn more about the topics introduced in this series.

- Challenge students with some of the more complex weeks by leading teacher-directed discussions of the vocabulary and concepts presented.

- Support students in practicing the varied types of questions asked throughout the practice pages.

- Extend your teaching of reading informational texts by using the texts in this book as instructional practice for close reading, responding to text-dependent questions, and providing evidence for answers.

How to Use This Book

180 Days of Social Studies offers teachers and parents a full page of social studies practice for each day of the school year.

Weekly Structure

These activities reinforce grade-level skills across a variety of social studies concepts. The content and questions are provided as full practice pages, making them easy to prepare and implement as part of a classroom routine or for homework.

Every practice page provides content, questions, and/or tasks that are tied to a social studies topic and standard. Students are given opportunities for regular practice in social studies, allowing them to build confidence through these quick standards-based activities.

Weekly Topics and Themes

The activities are organized by a weekly topic within one of the four social studies disciplines: history, civics, geography, and economics. The following chart shows the topics that are covered during each week of instruction:

Week	Discipline	Social Studies Topic	NCSS Theme
1	History	Past/present/future	Time, continuity, and change
2	Civics	Being a good citizen at school	Civic ideals and practices
3	Geography	Map and globe skills—Reading and locating in a classroom context	People, places, and environments
4	Economics	Wants and needs	Production, distribution, and consumption
5	History	Historic figures	Culture
6	Civics	Being a patriotic American	Culture
7	Geography	Map and globe skills—Reading maps and legends in a school context	People, places, and environments
8	Economics	Goods	Production, distribution, and consumption
9	History	Historic figures	Culture; Time, continuity, and change

How to Use This Book *(cont.)*

Week	Discipline	Social Studies Topic	NCSS Theme
10	Civics	Rules at school	Civic ideals and practices Individual development and identity
11	Geography	Map and globe skills—Reading maps and legends in a community context	People, places, and environments
12	Economics	Goods and services	Production, distribution, and consumption
13	History	Compare the lives of historic figures and people today	Culture; Time, continuity, and change
14	Civics	Rules at home	Civic ideals and practices; Individual development and identity
15	Geography	Map and globe skills—Reading and constructing maps	People, places, and environments
16	Economics	Producers and consumers	Production, distribution, and consumption
17	History	Compare the lives of recent historic figures and our lives today	Culture; Time, continuity, and change
18	Civics	People of power and authority at school and in the community	Civic ideals and practices; Power, authority, and governance
19	Geography	Map and globe skills—Reading and constructing community maps	People, places, and environments
20	Economics	Roles of community workers	Production, distribution, and consumption
21	History	Comparing life long ago with life today	People, places, and environments
22	Civics	Character traits of good citizens	Civic ideals and practices; Power, authority, and governance

How to Use This Book (cont.)

Week	Discipline	Social Studies Topic	NCSS Theme
23	Geography	Oceans, continents, and landforms	People, places, and environments
24	Economics	Roles of community workers	Production, distribution, and consumption
25	History	The impact of American Indians and immigrants	People, places, and environments
26	Civics	Being a patriotic citizen	Civic ideals and practices; Individual development and identity
27	Geography	People's responses to climate	People, places, and environments
28	Economics	How people get goods	Production, distribution, and consumption
29	History	Holidays and celebrations that reflect our history	Time, continuity, and change
30	Civics	Being a patriotic citizen—Landmarks	Civic ideals and practices; Individual development and identity
31	Geography	The environment	People, places, and environments
32	Economics	Why people earn money	Production, distribution, and consumption
33	History	Holidays and celebrations that reflect our history	Time, continuity, and change
34	Civics	Being a good citizen in the United States—Rights and responsibilities	Civic ideals and practices; Power, authority, and governance
35	Geography	People's responses to the environment	People, places, and environments
36	Economics	Children's jobs in the classroom	Production, distribution, and consumption

How to Use This Book *(cont.)*

Using the Practice Pages

Practice pages provide instruction and assessment opportunities for each day of the school year. Days 1 to 4 provide content in short texts or graphics followed by related questions or tasks. Day 5 provides an application task based on the week's work.

All four social studies disciplines are practiced. There are nine weeks of topics for each discipline. The discipline is indicated on the margin of each page.

Day 1: Students read a text about the weekly topic and answer questions. This day provides a general introduction to the week's topic.

Day 2: Students read a text and answer questions. Typically, this content is more specialized than Day 1.

Day 3: Students analyze a primary source or other graphic (chart, table, graph, or infographic) related to the weekly topic and answer questions.

How to Use This Book *(cont.)*

Using the Practice Pages *(cont.)*

Day 4: Students analyze an image or text and answer questions. Then, students make connections to their own lives.

Day 5: Students analyze a primary source or other graphic and respond to it using knowledge they've gained throughout the week. This day serves as an application of what they've learned.

Diagnostic Assessment

Teachers can use the practice pages as diagnostic assessments. The data analysis tools included with the book enable teachers or parents to quickly score students' work and monitor their progress. Teachers and parents can see which skills students may need to target further to develop proficiency.

Students will learn skills to support informational text analysis, primary source analysis, how to make connections to self, and how to apply what they learned. To assess students' learning in these areas, check their answers based on the answer key or use the *Response Rubric* (page 200) for constructed-response questions that you want to evaluate more deeply. Then, record student scores on the *Practice Page Item Analysis* (page 204). You may also wish to complete a *Student Item Analysis by Discipline* for each student (pages 206–207). These charts are also provided in the Digital Resources as PDFs, *Microsoft Word®* files, and *Microsoft Excel®* files. Teachers can input data into the electronic files directly on the computer, or they can print the pages. See page 208 for more information.

Diagnostic Assessment (cont.)

Practice Page Item Analyses

Every four weeks, follow these steps:

- Choose the four-week range you're assessing in the first row.

- Write or type the students' names in the far left column. Depending on the number of students, more than one copy of the form may be needed.

  - The skills are indicated across the top of the chart.

- For each student, record how many correct answers they gave and/or their rubric scores in the appropriate columns. There will be four numbers in each cell, one for each week. You can view which students are or are not understanding the social studies concepts or student progress after multiple opportunities to respond to specific text types or question forms.

- Review students' work for the first four sections. Add the scores for each student, and write that sum in the far right column. Use these scores as benchmarks to determine how each student is performing.

Student Item Analyses by Discipline

For each discipline, follow these steps:

- Write or type the student's name on the top of the charts.

  - The skills are indicated across the tops of the charts.

- Select the appropriate discipline and week.

- For each student, record how many correct answers they gave and/or their rubric scores in the appropriate columns. You can view which students are or are not understanding each social studies discipline or student progress after multiple opportunities to respond to specific text types or question forms.

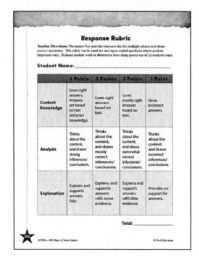

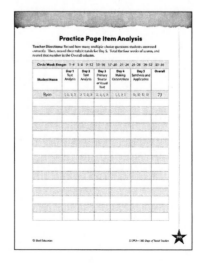

Using the Results to Differentiate Instruction

Once results are gathered and analyzed, teachers can use the results to inform the way they differentiate instruction. The data can help determine which social studies skills and content are the most difficult for students and which students need additional instructional support and continued practice. Depending on how often the practice pages are scored, results can be considered for instructional support on a weekly or monthly basis.

Whole-Class Support

The results of the diagnostic analysis may show that the entire class is struggling with a particular concept or group of concepts. If these concepts have been taught in the past, this indicates that further instruction or reteaching is necessary. If these concepts have not been taught in the past, this data is a great preassessment and demonstrate that students do not have a working knowledge of the concepts. Thus, careful planning for the length of the unit(s) or lesson(s) must be considered, and extra front-loading may be required.

Small-Group or Individual Support

The results of the diagnostic analysis may show that an individual or a small group of students is struggling with a particular concept or group of concepts. If these concepts have been taught in the past, this indicates that further instruction or reteaching is necessary. Consider pulling aside these students while others are working independently to instruct further on the concept(s). You can also use the result to help identify individuals or groups of proficient students who are ready for enrichment or above-grade-level instruction. These students may benefit from independent learning contracts or more challenging activities.

Digital Resources

The Digital Resources contain PDFs and editable digital copies of the rubrics and item analysis pages. See page 208 for more information.

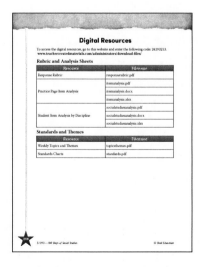

Standards Correlations

Shell Education is committed to producing educational materials that are research and standards based. In this effort, we have correlated all products to the academic standards of all 50 states, the District of Columbia, the Department of Defense Dependent Schools, and the Canadian provinces.

How to Find Standards Correlations

To print a customized correlation report of this product for your state, visit our website at **www.teachercreatedmaterials.com/administrators/correlations/** and follow the online directions. If you require assistance in printing correlation reports, please contact the Customer Service Department at 1-877-777-3450.

Purpose and Intent of Standards

The Every Student Succeeds Act (ESSA) mandates that all states adopt challenging academic standards that help students meet the goal of college and career readiness. While many states already adopted academic standards prior to ESSA, the act continues to hold states accountable for detailed and comprehensive standards.

Standards are designed to focus instruction and guide adoption of curricula. Standards are statements that describe the criteria necessary for students to meet specific academic goals. They define the knowledge, skills, and content students should acquire at each level. Standards are also used to develop standardized tests to evaluate students' academic progress. Teachers are required to demonstrate how their lessons meet state standards. State standards are used in the development of all of our products, so educators can be assured they meet the academic requirements of each state.

NCSS Standards and the C3 Framework

The lessons in this book are aligned to the National Council for the Social Studies (NCSS) standards and the C3 Framework. The chart on pages 5–7 lists the NCSS themes used throughout this book.

McREL Compendium

Each year, McREL analyzes state standards and revises the compendium to produce a general compilation of national standards. The chart on pages 13–14 correlates specific McREL standards to the content covered each week.

Standards Correlations *(cont.)*

Week	McREL Standard
1	Understands family life now and in the past, and family life in various places long ago.
2	Understands the sources, purposes, and functions of law, and the importance of the rule of law for the protection of individual rights and the common good.
3	Understands the characteristics and uses of maps, globes, and other geographic tools and technologies.
4	Understands basic features of market structures and exchanges.
5	Understands how democratic values came to be, and how they have been exemplified by people, events, and symbols.
6	Understands ideas about civic life, politics, and government.
7	Knows the location of places, geographic features, and patterns of the environment.
8	Understands basic features of market structures and exchanges.
9	Understands how democratic values came to be, and how they have been exemplified by people, events, and symbols.
10	Understands ideas about civic life, politics, and government.
11	Knows the location of places, geographic features, and patterns of the environment.
12	Understands basic features of market structures and exchanges.
13	Understands how democratic values came to be, and how they have been exemplified by people, events, and symbols.
14	Understands the sources, purposes, and functions of law, and the importance of the rule of law for the protection of individual rights and the common good.
15	Understands the physical and human characteristics of place Understands the nature and complexity of Earth's cultural mosaics.
16	Understands the roles government plays in the United States economy.
17	Understands family life now and in the past, and family life in various places long ago.
18	Understands ideas about civic life, politics, and government.
19	Understands the concept of regions Understands the physical and human characteristics of place.
20	Understands that scarcity of productive resources requires choices that generate opportunity costs.
21	Understands the folklore and other cultural contributions from various regions of the United States and how they helped to form a national heritage.
22	Understands ideas about civic life, politics, and government.

Standards Correlations *(cont.)*

Week	McREL Standard
23	Understands the physical and human characteristics of place. Understands the patterns of human settlement and their causes.
24	Understands that scarcity of productive resources requires choices that generate opportunity costs. Understands basic features of market structures and exchanges.
25	Understands the folklore and other cultural contributions from various regions of the United States and how they helped to form a national heritage.
26	Understands ideas about civic life, politics, and government.
27	Understands the physical and human characteristics of place. Understands how human actions modify the physical environment.
28	Understands that scarcity of productive resources requires choices that generate opportunity costs.
29	Understands major discoveries in science and technology, some of their social and economic effects, and the major scientists and inventors responsible for them.
30	Understands how certain character traits enhance citizens' ability to fulfill personal and civic responsibilities. Understands the roles of voluntarism and organized groups in American social and political life.
31	Understands the changes that occur in the meaning, use, distribution and importance of resources. Understands how human actions modify the physical environment.
32	Understands that scarcity of productive resources requires choices that generate opportunity costs.
33	Understands the history of a local community and how communities in North America varied long ago.
34	Understands how certain character traits enhance citizens' ability to fulfill personal and civic responsibilities.
35	Understands the characteristics and uses of spatial organization of Earth's surface. Understands the changes that occur in the meaning, use, distribution and importance of resources.
36	Understands that scarcity of productive resources requires choices that generate opportunity costs.

Name: _____ **Date:** _____

Directions: Look at the pictures. Read the text.

Babies Change

Babies grow. Babies change. They learn to go places.

First   **Next**   **Then**   **Last**

1. Which comes first?

  a.   **b.**   **c.**

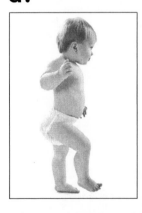  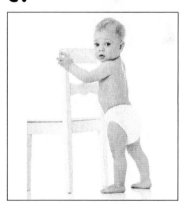

2. What do babies do?

  a. read

  b. write

  c. change

History

Name: _____ **Date:** _____

Directions: Look at the time line. Answer the questions.

A Person's Time Line

1. What age comes first?

a.

b.

c.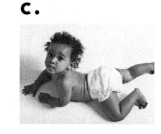

2. Where are you on the time line?

a.

b.

c.

Name: _____ **Date:** _____

Directions: Read the time line. Answer the questions.

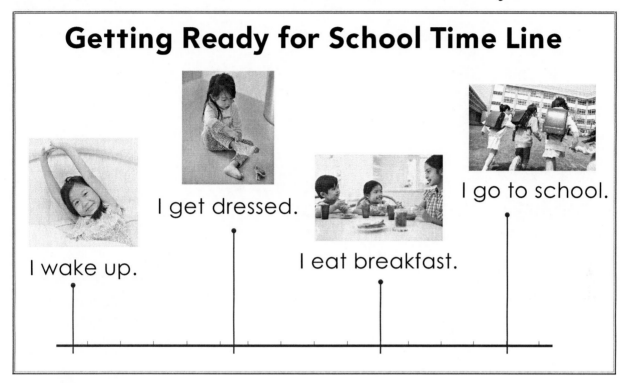

Getting Ready for School Time Line

I get dressed.

I go to school.

I wake up.

I eat breakfast.

1. What does this girl do before school?

   a. She eats lunch.

   b. She eats breakfast.

   c. She eats dinner.

2. Draw a picture of one thing you do before school.

Name: _____ **Date:** _____

Directions: Read the time line. Answer the questions.

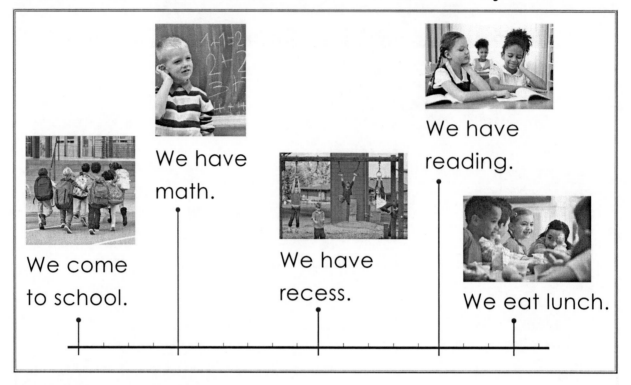

We have math.

We have reading.

We come to school.

We have recess.

We eat lunch.

1. When do they have lunch?
   a. before recess
   b. after reading
   c. before school

2. What would you add to this time line? Draw it.

Name: _____ **Date:** _____

Directions: Look at the time line. Draw to fill in the boxes.

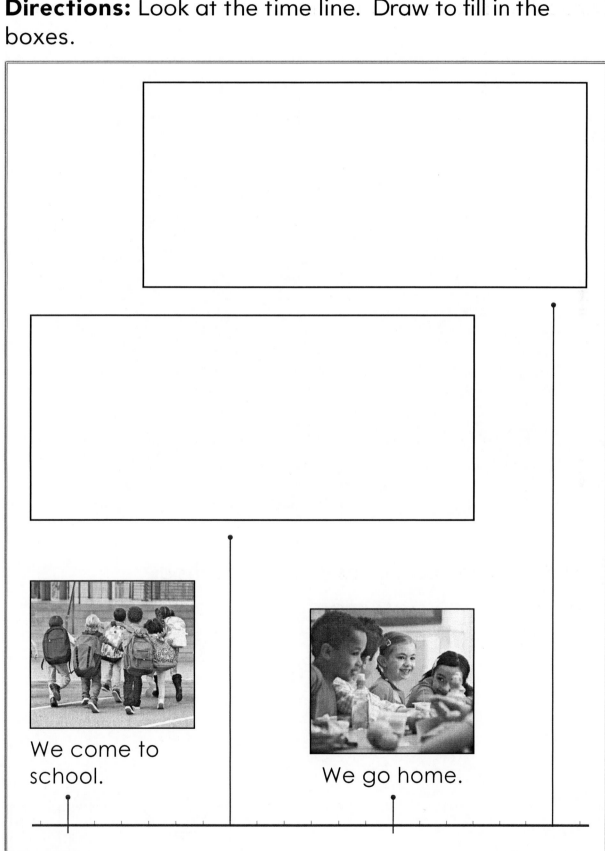

We come to school.

We go home.

Civics

Name: _____ **Date:** _____

Directions: Look at the picture. Read the text. Answer the questions.

Being a Good Citizen at School

We help each other at school. We listen. We share and take turns. We care for our class. We care for our school. We are good citizens at school.

1. How can you be a good citizen at school?

   a. Run in the classroom.

   b. Help each other.

   c. Stop listening to the teacher.

2. What are the students in the picture doing?

   a. sharing

   b. crying

   c. fighting

20

51393—180 Days of Social Studies

Name: _____ **Date:** _____

Directions: Look at the picture. Read the text. Answer the questions.

Listening

It is story time at school. The teacher reads a story.

1. What are the children doing?

   a. talking

   b. yawning

   c. listening

2. Who do we listen to at school?

   a. our lunches

   b. our teacher

   c. our pets

Civics

Name: _____ Date: _____

Directions: Look at the picture. Answer the questions.

Sharing and Taking Turns at School

1. What are the students sharing?

   a. snacks

   b. pencils

   c. clothes

2. How does sharing help the students create their art?

_____

_____

_____

_____

_____

51393—180 Days of Social Studies

Name: _____ **Date:** _____

Directions: Look at the picture. Read the text. Answer the questions.

Taking Care of Our School

We help keep our school and school yard clean.

1. What are the children doing?

   a. playing outside

   b. having a snack

   c. picking up trash

2. How do you help take care of your school? Draw a picture.

Name: _____ Date: _____

Directions: Look at the pictures. Circle the students who are being good citizens at school.

Civics

Name: _____ **Date:** _____

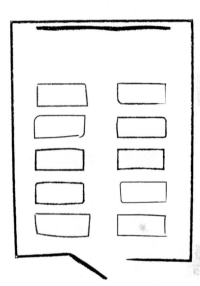

Directions: Look at the pictures. Read the text. Answer the questions.

This Is My Classroom

See my classroom. We have desks and chairs. We sit on the floor. We have a board. I made a map.

---

1. What is in this classroom?

   a. stove

   b. board

   c. slide

2. Where can students sit?

   a. on the floor

   b. on the shelf

   c. on the board

Geography

Name: _____ **Date:** _____

Directions: Look at the map. Answer the questions.

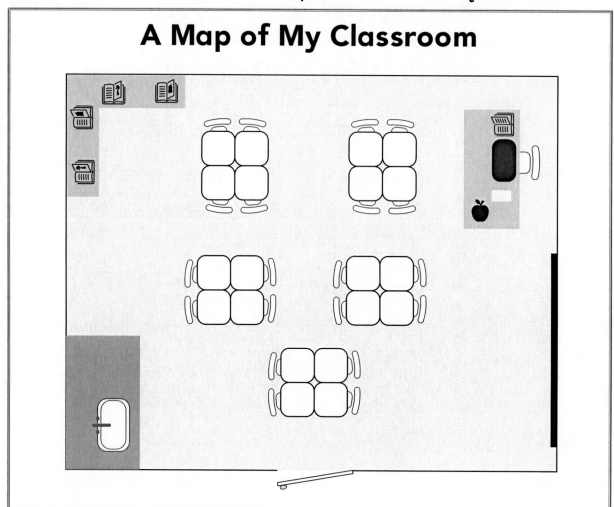

A Map of My Classroom

1. How many student desks do you see?

  a. 5

  b. 12

  c. 20

2. Where is the best place for students to keep books?

  a. on bookshelves

  b. in the sink

  c. at the door

Name: _____ **Date:** _____

Directions: Look at the map. Answer the questions.

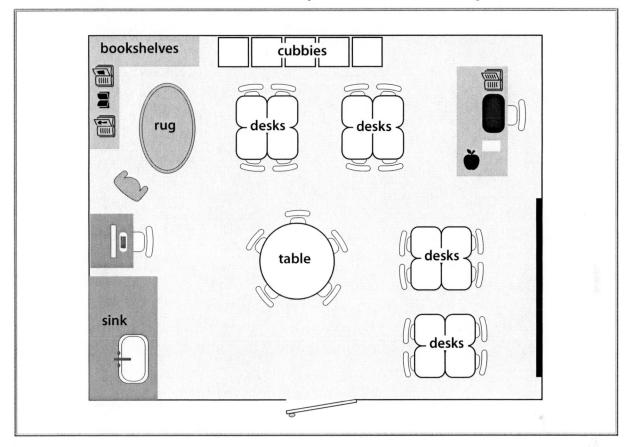

1. Where do students wash their hands after lunch?

   a. at the teacher's desk

   b. at the sink

   c. at the computer table

2. Where would you sit to hear a story? Why?

   _____

   _____

   _____

   _____

   _____

Name: _____ **Date:** _____

Geography

Directions: Look at the map. Answer the questions.

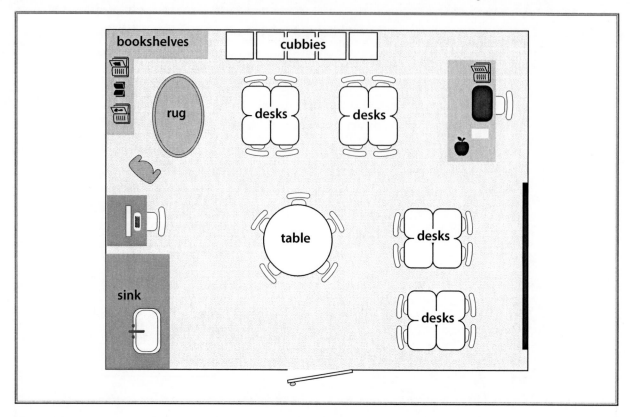

1. Circle places where students do their work.

2. What is in your classroom that is NOT on this map? Draw a picture.

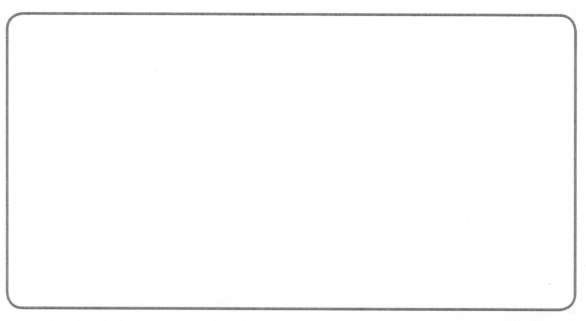

Name: _____ **Date:** _____

Directions: Look at the pictures. Pick a picture. Draw a map of the classroom.

Economics

Name: _____   **Date:** _____

Directions: Look at the picture. Read the text. Answer the questions.

Wants and Needs

We all need things. We need food and clothes. We need air and water and a place to live. We need these things to live.

Sometimes, we want things. We want toys and special clothes. We want our favorite things to eat and drink. These things help make us happy.

1. Circle TWO things that are wants.

   a. toys

   b. games

   c. air

2. Based on the text, why must we get all our needs?

   a. They make us unhappy.

   b. We can't live without them.

   c. They cost us money.

Name: _____ **Date:** _____

Directions: Look at the picture. Read the text. Answer the questions.

A Family Dinner

This boy eats dinner with his family. He needs his food. He needs a drink. He is happy.

1. What does this boy need?

    a. ice cream

    b. bicycle

    c. healthy food

2. What does this boy want?

    a. ice cream

    b. apple

    c. glass of water

Economics

Name: _____ **Date:** _____

Directions: Look at the pictures. Read the text. Draw a picture in each box. Label your pictures.

Things That Make Us Happy

Some things we
need make us happy.

Some things we
want make us happy.

Something I Need That Makes Me Happy	Something I Want That Makes Me Happy

51393—180 Days of Social Studies   © Shell Education

Name: _____ **Date:** _____

Directions: Read the story. Answer the questions. You can write or draw.

> Amy was walking home from school. It began to rain. She began to run. Then, she heard thunder. There was lightning.
>
> She ran in the house. She hugged her mom. Her mom told Amy they were safe. Amy was all wet!

1. What does Amy need? What does Amy want?

Needs	Wants

51393—180 Days of Social Studies

Name: _____ **Date:** _____

Economics

Directions: Look at the chart. Fill in the missing words or pictures.

Needs	Wants
She needs warm clothes.	She wants a purple jacket.
She needs a healthy drink.	She wants _____.
He needs a _____.	He wants a _____.

Name: _____ **Date:** _____

Directions: Look at the picture. Read the text. Answer the questions.

History

People Made the USA

We live in the USA. Many people have lived in the USA. Long ago, people helped m ake the USA.

---

1. Where do we live?

  a. We live in Europe.

  b. We live in the USA.

  c. We live in Africa.

2. What does the author say people did long ago?

  a. They made the USA.

  b. They went to the store.

  c. They painted pictures.

History

Name: _____ **Date:** _____

Directions: Look at the picture. Read the text. Answer the questions.

Squanto

Squanto helped the Pilgrims. He showed them how to hunt. He showed them how to plant.

1. Based on the text, who did Squanto help?

a. lost people

b. his pets

c. the Pilgrims

2. What did Squanto teach the Pilgrims?

a. how to sleep

b. how to plant

c. how to eat

Name: _____ **Date:** _____

Directions: Look at the picture. Answer the questions.

Harriet Tubman Helped People Be Free

1. What did Tubman do?
   a. She helped people be free.
   b. She left the United States.
   c. She took people back home.

2. How did people feel when Tubman helped them? Use words and a picture.

_____

_____

_____

_____

History

Name: _____ **Date:** _____

Directions: Look at the picture. Read the text. Answer the questions.

Francis Scott Key

Francis Scott Key saw the flag long ago. He was happy. He wrote a poem about the flag.

1. Why did Key write a poem?

   a. He liked to write.

   b. He saw the flag.

   c. He was sad.

2. Look at the two flags. How are they the same? How are they different?

_____

_____

_____

_____

_____

51393—180 Days of Social Studies   © *Shell Education*

Name: _____ **Date:** _____

Directions: Read the text. Cut apart the names. Glue them in the correct boxes.

People Helped Make the United States	
This person wrote a poem. This person loved the flag. Who was this person?	
This person helped people. They wanted to be free. Who was this person?	
This person showed how to plant. This person showed how to hunt. Who was this person?	

Harriet Tubman	Francis Scott Key	Squanto

Name: _____ **Date:** _____

Civics

Directions: Look at the pictures. Read the text. Answer the questions.

Being a Patriotic Citizen

We sing songs. We sing our songs together. There are songs about our flag. There are songs about our country. We are proud of our country.

 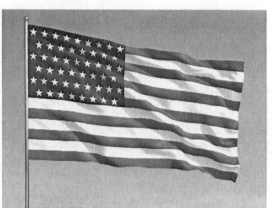

1. What are the children doing?
   a. eating together
   b. singing together
   c. walking together

2. What are patriotic songs about?
   a. our animals
   b. our houses
   c. our country

Name: _____ **Date:** _____

Directions: Look at the pictures. Read the text. Answer the questions.

"America the Beautiful"

We sing a song about America. Our country is beautiful. We have big skies. We have fields. We have mountains and seas.

---

1. What is a beautiful thing in the text?

   a. the mountains

   b. the turtles

   c. the motorcycles

2. What is the name of the song?

   a. "A Beautiful Country"

   b. "America the Beautiful"

   c. "I Love America"

Civics

Name: _____ **Date:** _____

Directions: Look at the pictures. Answer the questions.

"The Star-Spangled Banner" Is Our Anthem

...the land of the free and the home of the brave ♪♫♪

1. What are they singing?

a. a sad song

b. a funny song

c. our anthem

2. What do you do when you sing our anthem? Draw a picture of you singing.

Name: _____ **Date:** _____

Directions: Look at the pictures. Read the text.
Answer the questions.

We Sing Songs about America

We sing songs at school. We sing songs at ball games. We sing songs at Fourth of July parades.

---

1. Based on the words, where do we sing songs about America?

   a. in the closet

   b. at the dentist

   c. at school

2. Where else do you want to sing a song about America?

   _____

   _____

   _____

   _____

   _____

Name: _____ **Date:** _____

Civics

Directions: Cut apart the pictures. Glue them with the matching words.

our flag
fields of grain
sea
mountain
We sing.

Name: _____ **Date:** _____

Directions: Look at the map. Read the text. Answer the questions.

This Is My Classroom

Here is a map of my classroom. Some things are missing. We have desks. We have shelves. We have computers. We sit on the floor to hear a story. We have a door and windows.

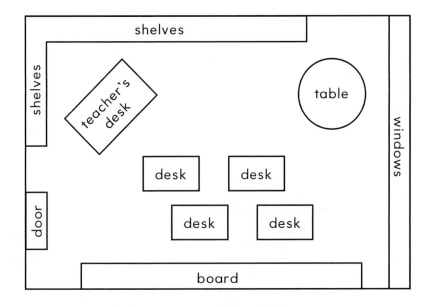

---

1. What is missing on the map?

   a. desks

   b. computers

   c. door

2. In this classroom, what is near the windows?

   a. teacher's desk

   b. table

   c. door

Name: _____ **Date:** _____

Geography

Directions: Look at the map. Read the text. Answer the questions.

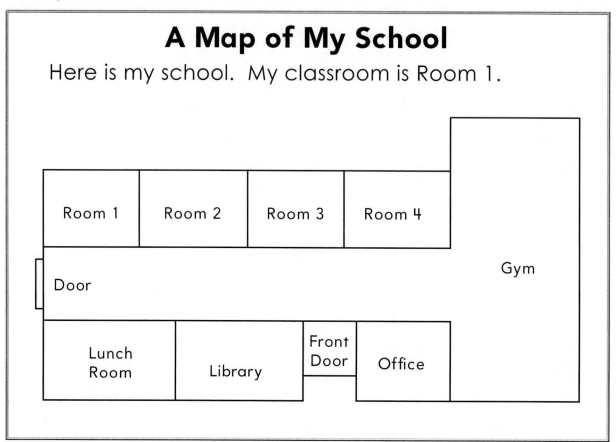

A Map of My School

Here is my school. My classroom is Room 1.

| Room 1 | Room 2 | Room 3 | Room 4 |

Door

Gym

| Lunch Room | Library | Front Door | Office |

1. What is across the hall from my room?

   a. office

   b. front door

   c. lunch room

2. What classroom is beside the gym?

   a. Room 4

   b. the library

   c. Room 2

Name: _____ **Date:** _____

Directions: Look at the picture and map. Answer the questions.

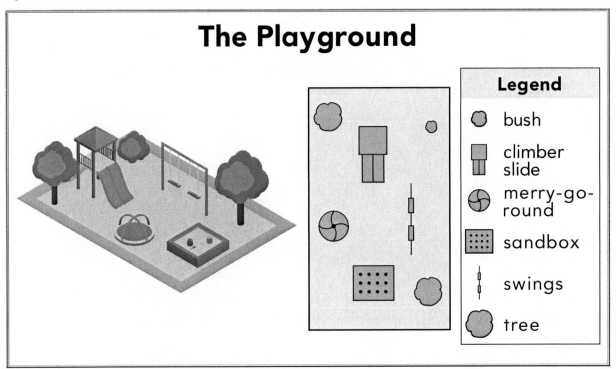

The Playground

Legend

bush

climber slide

merry-go-round

sandbox

swings

tree

1. Which symbol means a sandbox?

a.

b.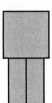

c.

2. What does this symbol mean?

   a. climber slide

   b. merry-go-round

   c. tree

Name: _____ **Date:** _____

Geography

Directions: Look at the picture and map. Answer the questions.

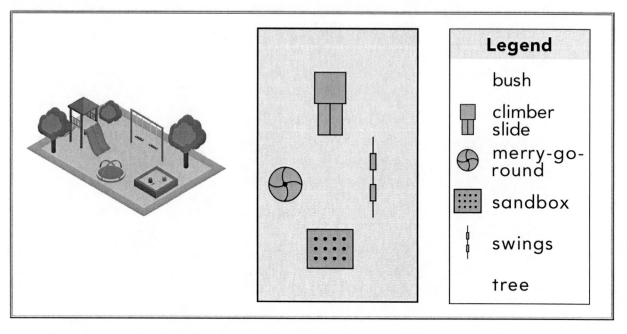

1. Put the two missing symbols on the map and the legend.

2. Where would you like to play in this playground? Draw the symbol.

Name: _____ **Date:** _____

Directions: Look at the picture and map. Draw the symbols in the legend.

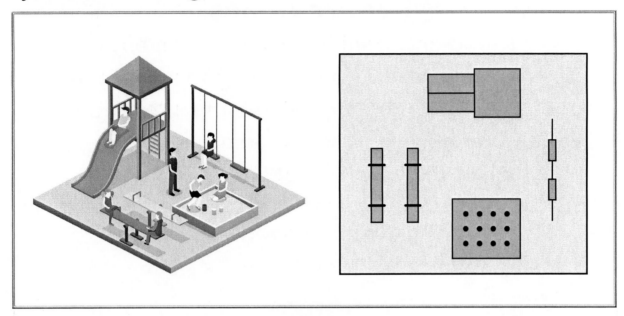

Legend

climber slide

sandbox

seesaw

swings

Economics

Name: _____ Date: _____

Directions: Read the text. Answer the questions.

What Are Goods?

We all need and want things. If we can buy or trade these things, they are called *goods*. We use goods every day. Some goods we use over and over, such as clothes or books. Some goods we use once, such as the food we eat.

1. Circle TWO things that are goods.

   a. cell phone   **b.** game   **c.** sun

2. Circle TWO places where you can get goods.

   a. grocery store   **b.** moon   **c.** garage sale

51393—180 Days of Social Studies   © *Shell Education*

Name: _____ **Date:** _____

Directions: Look at the picture. Read the text. Answer the questions.

Goods in Our Classroom

We use goods in our classroom. Some goods we use many times. Some goods we use a few times. Some goods we use once.

1. Which good CANNOT be used many times?

a. scissors   **b.** apple   **c.** pencil

2. Circle TWO reasons why we can't use goods forever.

a. Some will break.

b. Some will fly away.

c. Some will be eaten.

Economics

Name: _____ **Date:** _____

Directions: Find FIVE different goods in the picture. Place an **X** on each good. Then, finish the sentences.

1. Two goods we **need** in our classroom are

_____

– –

_____

2. Two goods we **want** in our classroom are

_____

– –

_____

Name: _____ **Date:** _____

Directions: We need goods at home. Draw a good you might find in each room.

Economics

Goods at Home

Bedroom	Kitchen
Living Room or Family Room	**Bathroom**

Economics

Name: _____ **Date:** _____

Directions: Read the story. Draw the goods from the story.

Emma and Her Father Go Shopping

Emma and her father went shopping. They walked down the street. They said hello to Mrs. Chen. They walked by a toy store. Emma saw a toy truck.

Emma and her father went to the grocery store. They had two bags. Emma had carrots, lettuce, and bread. Her father had eggs, cookies, and apples. He also had milk.

When they got home, they put their groceries on the kitchen table. They ate some cookies.

51393—180 Days of Social Studies

Name: _____ **Date:** _____

Directions: Look at the picture. Read the text. Answer the questions.

Going to Space

We live in the United States. We go to space. We learn about space. Neil Armstrong was the first man on the moon. Our flag is on the moon now.

1. Where does the author say Armstrong went?

   a. to Canada

   b. to a mountain

   c. to the moon

2. What did he put on the moon?

   a. our flag

   b. a box

   c. a house

History

Name: _____ Date: _____

Directions: Look at the picture. Read the text. Answer the questions.

Mae C. Jemison

Mae C. Jemison lives in the United States. She went to space. She was an astronaut.

1. Where does the author say Jemison went?
   a. for a walk
   b. to space
   c. in the house

2. Where does Jemison live?
   a. in the United States
   b. in Japan
   c. in Canada

3. Draw Jemison in space.

Name: _____ **Date:** _____

Directions: Look at the picture. Answer the questions.

Thomas Edison Invented Light Bulbs

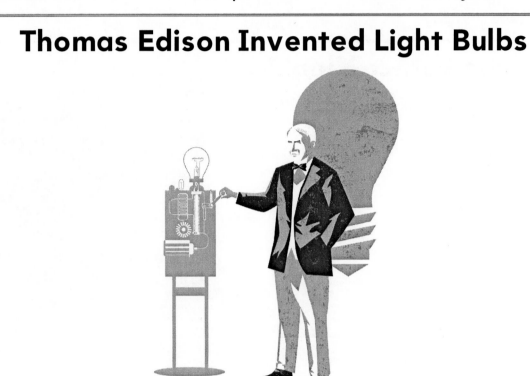

---

1. What was Thomas Edison?

   a. an actor

   b. an inventor

   c. a tailor

2. Why are light bulbs important?

_____

_____

_____

_____

History

Name: _____ **Date:** _____

Directions: Look at the picture. Read the text. Answer the questions.

Martin Luther King Jr.

Martin Luther King Jr. had a dream. He told people his dream. He wanted us to be fair. He wanted us to be friends.

1. What did King want?

    a. He wanted people to be mean.

    b. He wanted people to be fair.

    c. He wanted people to be sad.

2. Draw how you could make King proud of you.

Name: _____ **Date:** _____

Directions: Read the text. Cut apart the names. Glue them in the correct boxes.

People in the United States	
This person had a dream. This person wanted us to be fair. Who was this person?	
This person walked on the moon. This person put a flag on the moon. Who was this person?	
This person went to space. This person was a woman. Who was this person?	
This person was an inventor. He invented light bulbs.	

✂

Thomas Edison	Mae C. Jemison	Martin Luther King Jr.	Neil Armstrong

Civics

Name: _____ **Date:** _____

Directions: Read the text. Answer the questions.

Why We Have Rules

We have rules at school. We have rules at home. Rules tell us what we may do. They tell us what we should not do. Rules keep us safe. Rules help us work and play.

1. Why do we have rules?

   a. They make us cry.

   b. They keep us safe.

   c. They make us fight.

2. What does the author say might happen if you don't know the rules?

   a. You might not be safe.

   b. You might make new friends.

   c. You might be hungry.

3. Draw yourself following a rule.

51393—180 Days of Social Studies

Name: _____ **Date:** _____

Directions: Look at the picture. Read the text. Answer the questions.

We Made Rules

We made rules in my class. Our teacher helped us.

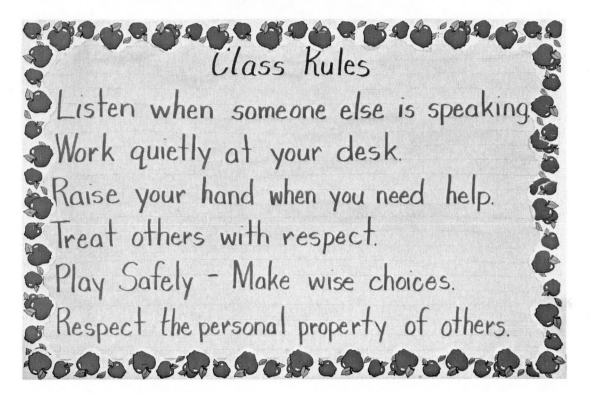

Class Rules
Listen when someone else is speaking.
Work quietly at your desk.
Raise your hand when you need help.
Treat others with respect.
Play Safely – Make wise choices.
Respect the personal property of others.

1. When do I listen?

   a. when I am talking out loud

   b. when I play tic-tac-toe

   c. when someone else is speaking

2. How should students play?

   a. sadly

   b. safely

   c. slowly

Civics

Name: _____ **Date:** _____

Directions: Look at the picture. Answer the questions.

Following Rules

1. What is a rule when the teacher is reading a story?

   a. Listen to the teacher.

   b. Talk to your friend.

   c. Look behind you.

2. Why is listening an important rule?

   _____

   _____

   _____

   _____

   _____

51393—180 Days of Social Studies

© *Shell Education*

Name: _____ **Date:** _____

Directions: Look at the chart. Answer the questions.

Civics

> # CLASS RULES
> Use your inside voice.
> Listen.
> Keep hands to self.
> Share.

1. How do the rules help us be safe and learn?

_____

_____

_____

_____

2. What rule would you add to the chart?

_____

_____

Name: _____ **Date:** _____

Directions: Look at the pictures. Read the text. Match the pictures to the rules.

Civics

Raise your hand.

Keep hands to self.

Listen.

Work hard.

Use walking feet.

51393—180 Days of Social Studies   © *Shell Education*

Name: _____ **Date:** _____

Directions: Look at the map. Read the text. Answer the questions.

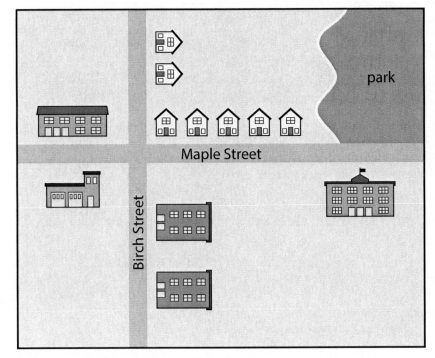

My Community

This is a map of my neighborhood.

Legend

apartment building

fire hall

house

library

park

school

Maple Street

Birch Street

park

1. What is across from my school?

   a. fire hall

   b. library

   c. park

2. What street has apartment buildings?

   a. Red Street

   b. Blue Street

   c. no street

Geography

Name: _____ **Date:** _____

Directions: Look at the map. Read the text. Answer the questions.

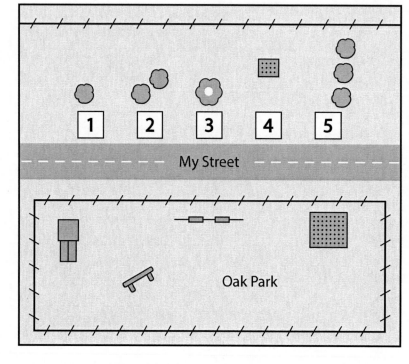

My Street

This is a map of my street. I live in house 5.

1. Which house has a sandbox?

a. house 1

b. house 4

c. house 5

2. What TWO things are found in the park?

a. swings

b. bench

c. fountain

Name: _____ **Date:** _____

Directions: Look at the map. Answer the questions.

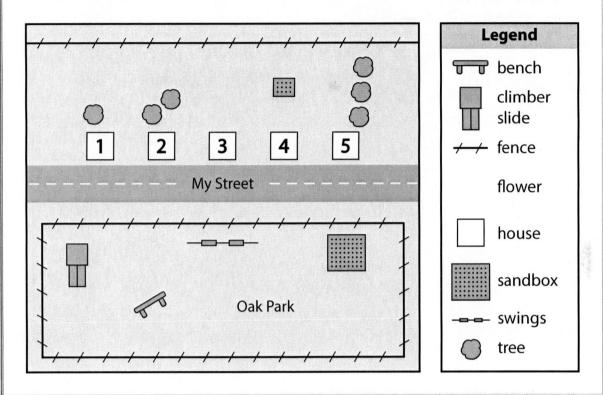

1. Color the fences blue.

2. Put a flower symbol in the legend. Draw flowers in the park and near house 3.

3. How many houses are there?

   a. 5

   b. 3

   c. 4

4. Draw more trees near the houses.

Geography

Name: _____ **Date:** _____

Directions: Look at the picture and legend . Answer the questions.

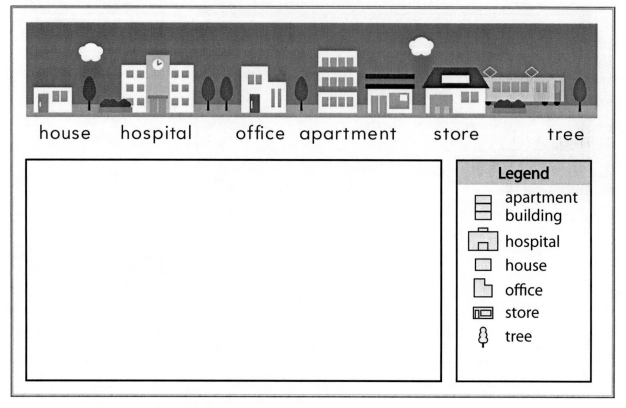

house   hospital   office   apartment   store   tree

Legend

	apartment building
	hospital
	house
	office
	store
	tree

1. Draw a map of this street.

2. Draw a new building for this street.

Name: _____ **Date:** _____

Directions: Look at the picture. Draw symbols that could be used on a map.

store   tree   post office   fire hall

Legend

fire hall

post office

store

tree

Economics

Name: _____ **Date:** _____

Directions: Read the text. Answer the questions.

What Are Goods and Services?

Goods are things we can buy or trade. A service is something a person does for you. Many people do services. Some people drive buses, cut hair, or look after sick people. There are many different goods and services.

1. Circle TWO jobs that sell or trade goods.

   a. farmer   **b.** pilot   **c.** car salesperson

2. Circle the TWO jobs that sell or trade services.

   a. taxi driver   **b.** garbage collector   **c.** baker

Name: _____ **Date:** _____

Directions: Look at the picture. Read the text. Answer the questions.

Services at School

Adults give services to children in school. Some adults teach children. Some adults help children when they get hurt or sick. Some adults keep the school clean.

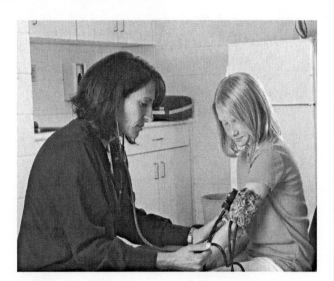

1. Circle TWO people who give services at school.

a. boat driver   **b.** custodian   **c.** teacher

2. A nurse gives many services. Circle TWO services a nurse gives.

a. helping a child who gets hurt

b. helping a child who is sad

c. helping a child to play baseball

Economics

Name: _____ **Date:** _____

Directions: Look at the poster. Circle the goods in red and the services in blue. Answer the questions.

Help Mr. Lopez's Class Raise Money for the Food Bank

Please help us raise money for the food bank.

What do you want?

10 chocolate chip cookies $2

student to clean up your book boxes $1

apple 50 cents

people to pick up trash in the playground $2

student to wipe off your boards $1

student to sharpen pencils $1

1. What other service could the students give?

_____

_____

_____

2. What other good could the students give?

_____

_____

_____

Name: _____ **Date:** _____

Directions: Read the text. Compare your services at home with Will's services.

Economics

Services at Home

My name is Will. I do services at home. Here is what I do. I make my bed. I clean up my toys. I feed my pets. I set the table. I take my dishes to the sink.

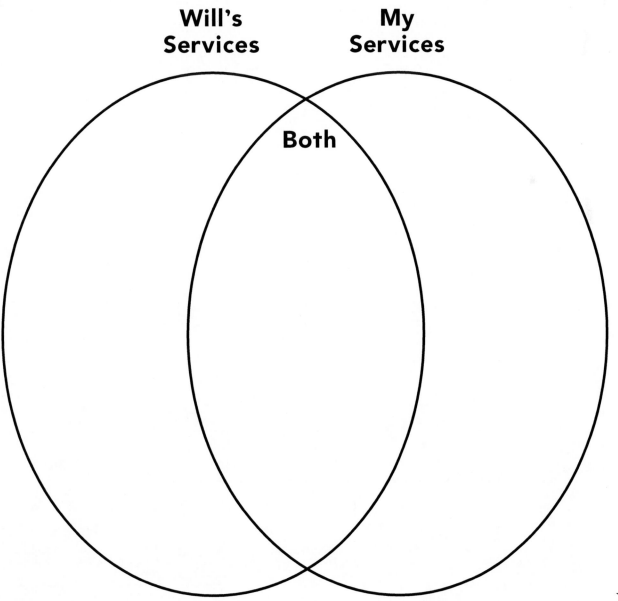

Will's Services

My Services

Both

Economics

Name: _____ **Date:** _____

Directions: Look at the pictures. Cut them apart. Glue them in the correct columns.

Goods	Services

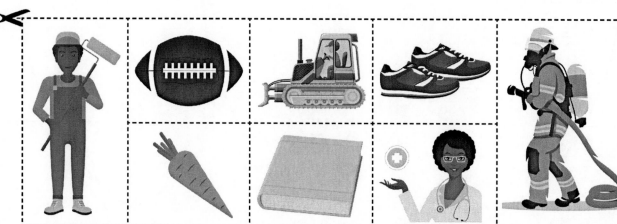

51393—180 Days of Social Studies

Name: _____ **Date:** _____

Directions: Look at the picture. Read the text. Answer the questions.

Abraham Lincoln

Abraham Lincoln lived long ago. He lived in a log cabin. It was hard to go to school. He worked hard.

1. When did Lincoln live?

  a. long ago

  b. now

  c. soon

2. When do you live?

  a. long ago

  b. now

  c. soon

History

Name: _____ **Date:** _____

Directions: Look at the picture. Read the text. Answer the questions.

Rebecca Boone

Rebecca Boone worked hard. She looked after the children. She cooked. She made clothes. Her husband hunted.

1. What did Boone do?

a. She cooked on a fire.

b. She wrote many books.

c. She played video games.

2. Where did Boone live?

a. in a big house

b. in a log cabin

c. in an apartment

Name: _____ **Date:** _____

Directions: Look at the picture. Answer the questions.

Squanto's Home

longhouse

wood

bark

1. What was a longhouse made of?

   a. bricks and wood

   b. bark and wood

   c. plastic and wood

2. Draw your home.

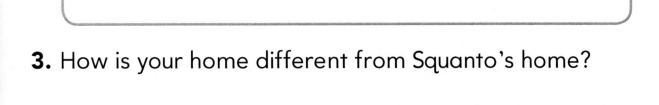

3. How is your home different from Squanto's home?

_____

_____

_____

Name: _____ **Date:** _____

Directions: Look at the picture. Read the text. Answer the questions.

History

Orville Wright

Orville Wright made the first airplane in the United States. He worked with his brother.

1. What did Wright make?

   a. the first car

   b. the first house

   c. the first airplane

2. What do airplanes look like today? Draw a picture.

Name: _____ **Date:** _____

Directions: Read the text. Cut apart the pictures. Glue them in the correct boxes.

People lived here long ago. Some things were the same. Some things were different.

What is the same?	What is different?

Civics

Name: _____ **Date:** _____

Directions: Look at the picture. Read the text. Answer the questions.

Rules at Home

Rules tell us what we may do. Rules tell us what we should not do. We have rules at school. We have rules at home. Rules keep us safe.

1. Why do we have rules?
   a. They make us sad.
   b. They help keep us safe.
   c. They help us fight.

2. Based on the text, what could happen if you break a rule?
   a. You might do something you should not do.
   b. You might fix something.
   c. You might be sleepy.

3. Based on the text, where are TWO places that we have rules?
   a. at school
   b. on the ocean floor
   c. at home

Name: _____ **Date:** _____

Directions: Look at the picture. Read the text. Answer the questions.

Rules and Laws

We have rules at school. We have rules at home. We have community rules. They are called *laws*. They tell us what we should do. They tell us what we should not do. They keep us safe.

1. What are laws?

   a. rules for playing games

   b. rules for singing songs

   c. rules in the community

2. Based on the text, how do laws help us?

   a. They keep us lonely.

   b. They keep us busy.

   c. They keep us safe.

Name: _____ **Date:** _____

Directions: Read the poster. Answer the questions.

Civics

OUR FAMILY RULES

1. Clean up.

2. Help each other.

3. Say please and thank you.

4. Be kind.

5. Go to bed on time.

6. Love each other.

1. What rules are on the poster?
   a. school rules
   b. park rules
   c. family rules

2. Which rule is the most important rule? Why?

   _____
   _____
   _____
   _____
   _____

51393—180 Days of Social Studies

© *Shell Education*

Name: _____ **Date:** _____

Directions: Look at the picture. Read the text. Answer the questions.

Taking Care of Our Things at School

We take care of our things at school. We put them away. We respect other people's things. We do not take other people's things. We are good friends.

1. Why don't we take other people's things?

_____

_ _

_____

2. How do you take care of your things at school?

_____

_ _

_____

Civics

Name: _____ **Date:** _____

Directions: Look at the pictures. Answer the question.

1. How do rules help make school and home better?

_____

- -

_____

_____

- -

_____

Name: _____ **Date:** _____

Directions: Read the text. Look at the legend. Answer the questions.

Mapping My Classroom

I am going to make a map. First, I think about my classroom. Next, I think about the legend. What goes on my legend? I think about symbols. Finally, I make my map.

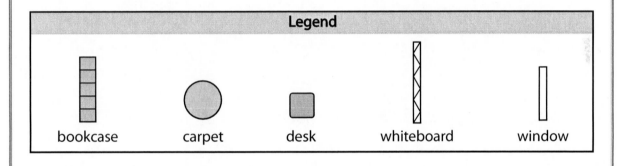

1. What should be added to the legend?

   a. stove

   b. roof

   c. door

2. Draw a symbol on the legend for your answer to question 1.

3. What does this symbol mean?

   a. sandbox

   b. carpet

   c. moon

Name: _____ **Date:** _____

Directions: Look at the map. Answer the questions.

Geography

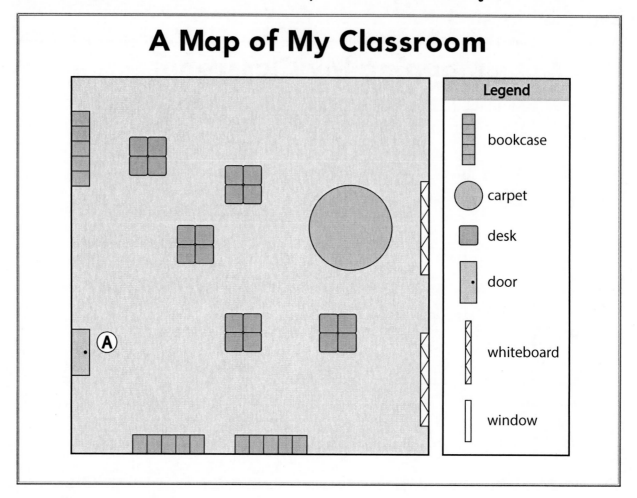

A Map of My Classroom

Legend
- bookcase
- carpet
- desk
- door
- whiteboard
- window

1. What symbol is at **A**?
   a. bookcase
   b. door
   c. desk

2. Look at the legend. What is NOT shown on the map?
   a. bookcase
   b. window
   c. door

Name: _____ **Date:** _____

Directions: Think about your classroom. Think of symbols. Make a legend. Draw a map.

My Classroom

Geography

Legend

desk or table

door

window

shelf

Geography

Name: _____ **Date:** _____

Directions: Think about your bedroom. Make a legend. Draw a map.

My Bedroom

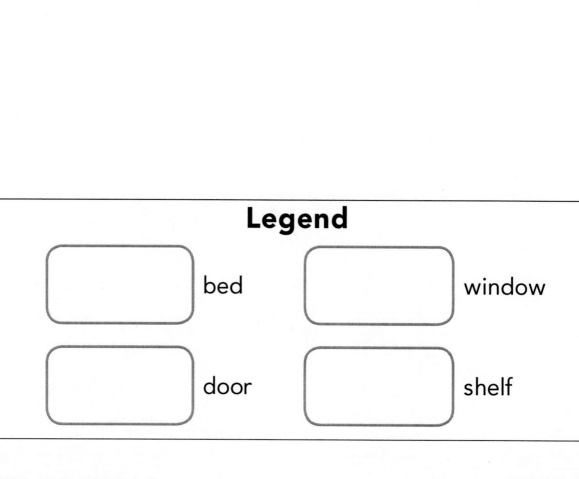

Legend

bed

window

door

shelf

Name: _____ **Date:** _____

Directions: Read the text. Make a legend. Draw a map.

> You are planning a new playground for your school. What is in your playground? Draw a map of the playground.

Our Playground

Legend

Economics

Name: _____ **Date:** _____

Directions: Look at the picture. Read the text. Answer the questions.

What Are Producers and Consumers?

Producers give services or make goods. Consumers buy or use the goods and services. Consumers and producers help each other.

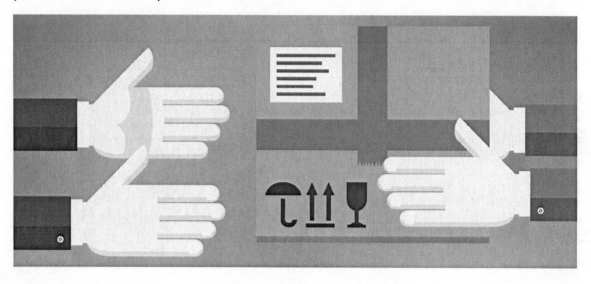

1. Based on the text, what can producers and consumers do?

   a. argue with each other

   b. help each other

   c. ignore each other

2. Why are consumers important?

   a. They like to walk around.

   b. They need goods and services.

   c. They like to sing.

Name: _____ **Date:** _____

Directions: Look at the picture. Read the text. Answer the questions.

Going to the Market

People go to the market. The market is a busy place. People can buy goods and services. This is a market in Malaysia.

---

1. Where is this market?

  a. Missouri

  b. Malaysia

  c. Mississippi

2. What goods and services is the woman selling?

  a. sewing and selling clothes

  b. cutting hair and selling combs

  c. cooking and serving food

Economics

Name: _____ **Date:** _____

Directions: Look at the picture. Answer the questions.

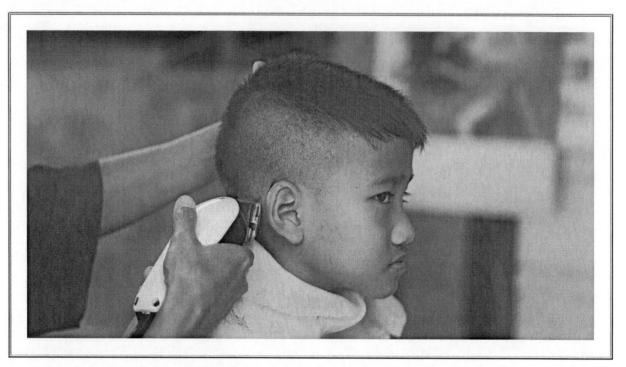

1. What service do you see in the picture?

   a. playing games

   b. cooking dinner

   c. cutting hair

2. What goods does the producer need to do this service?

_____

- -

_____

- -

_____

Name: _____ **Date:** _____

Directions: Read the text. Answer the questions.

Economics

Consumers and Producers at Home

Katya is a consumer and a producer at home. She eats dinner. She helps wash the dishes.

1. Draw or write three goods or services you consume at home.

2. Draw or write two goods or services you produce at home.

Economics

Name: _____ **Date:** _____

Directions: Look at the pictures. Circle the correct pictures. Put an **X** on each mistake.

Producers

Name: _____ **Date:** _____

Directions: Look at the picture. Read the text. Answer the questions.

Neil Armstrong and the Space Station

When Neil Armstrong was a boy, no one went to space. There was no space station.

Armstrong went to space. He went to the moon. Now there is a space station. The space station goes around Earth.

1. Where does the space station go?
   a. to the sun
   b. around Earth
   c. to the moon

2. Where did Armstrong go?
   a. He went to the bottom of the sea.
   b. He went to space.
   c. He went to the sun.

History

Name: _____ **Date:** _____

Directions: Look at the picture. Read the text. Answer the questions.

Unfair Rules

When Martin Luther King Jr. was a boy, the rules were not fair. African American children could not use the same restrooms as white children. They could not use the same doors. They could not drink from the same fountains. They could not go to the same schools. King helped change the rules.

1. What rule was not fair?
   a. Children could not use the same restrooms.
   b. Children could go in the same door.
   c. Children could eat with friends.

2. What did King do?
   a. He became president.
   b. He helped change the rules.
   c. He left the United States.

Name: _____ **Date:** _____

Directions: Look at the pictures. Answer the questions.

School Then

School Today

1. What makes the pictures the same?

_____

_ _

_____

_ _

_____

2. What makes the pictures different?

_____

_ _

_____

_ _

_____

History

Name: _____ **Date:** _____

Directions: Look at the picture. Read the text. Answer the questions.

Ruby Bridges

Ruby Bridges is an African American. When she was young, the laws were not fair. She could not go to the same schols as white children. She helped change the laws.

Today, all children can go to school together. They can be classmates.

1. What did Bridges do?

a. She stayed at home.

b. She thought the laws were fair.

c. She helped change the laws.

2. Share a rule from your family that is fair.

_____

_____

_____

_____

Name: _____ **Date:** _____

Directions: Look at the picture. Read the text. Answer the question.

These children live in the United States. The United States is changing. It is more fair now.

1. How has the United States become more fair? Draw a picture and write.

_____

- - - - - - - - - - - - - -

_____

_____

- - - - - - - - - - - - - -

_____

Civics

Name: _____ Date: _____

Directions: Look at the picture. Read the text. Answer the questions.

Our Teacher

Adults help us. They teach us. They help us learn. They keep us safe. We listen to adults. In our classroom, our teacher is the leader. We listen to our teacher.

1. Based on the text, who do we listen to?
   a. little babies
   b. young children
   c. adults

2. Based on the text, who is the leader in our classroom?
   a. Our teacher is the leader.
   b. My best friend is the leader.
   c. I am the leader.

Name: _____ **Date:** _____

Directions: Look at the picture. Read the text. Answer the questions.

The Principal

The principal is the school leader. She helps the teachers. She helps the children. She tells us the rules. We listen to her.

1. Based on the text, who helps the teachers?
   a. the painter
   b. the doctor
   c. the principal

2. How does the principal in the picture feel?
   a. She is angry.
   b. She is happy.
   c. She is tired.

Civics

Name: _____ **Date:** _____

Directions: Look at the picture. Read the text. Answer the questions.

Police Officers

1. Based on the picture, what do police officers do?

   a. They help keep us safe.

   b. They sweep the roads.

   c. They dance in the street.

2. What do you think the boy and the police officer are saying to each other?

   _____

   _____

   _____

   _____

   _____

102

Name: _____ **Date:** _____

Directions: Look at the pictures. Read the text. Answer the questions.

> We listen to the grown-ups. Grown-ups keep us safe at home.
>
>

1. Who are the grown-ups in your home?

_____

- - - - - - - - - - - - - - - - - - - -

_____

- - - - - - - - - - - - - - - - - - - -

_____

2. Why do we listen to grown-ups at home?

_____

- - - - - - - - - - - - - - - - - - - -

_____

- - - - - - - - - - - - - - - - - - - -

_____

Civics

Name: _____ **Date:** _____

Directions: Look at the pictures. Circle the grown-up leaders. Answer the question.

1. Pick one picture. Tell why this grown-up is a leader.

_____

_____

_____

_____

_____

_____

_____

51393—180 Days of Social Studies

Name: _____ **Date:** _____

Directions: Look at the map. Read the text. Answer the questions.

Finding My Way

I made a map of my neighborhood. I made a legend. I made a compass rose. It shows the directions. The directions are north, south, east, and west. They help us find things on the map.

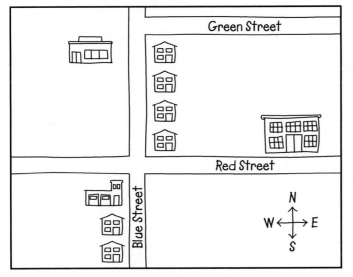

1. Which street is north of Red Street?
   a. Blue Street
   b. Green Street
   c. Black Street

2. What is south of the fire hall?
   a. store
   b. school
   c. houses

Geography

Name: _____ **Date:** _____

Directions: Look at the map. Read the text. Answer the questions.

My Neighborhood

My neighborhood has space to build at spots A, B, and C. I want to build houses south of the school.

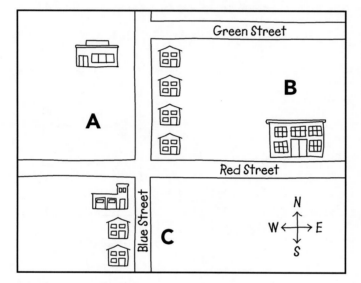

1. Which spot is south of the school?

   a. A

   b. B

   c. C

2. What street will the new houses be on?

   a. Blue Street

   b. Green Street

   c. Red Street

51393—180 Days of Social Studies

Name: _____ **Date:** _____

Directions: Look at the map. Answer the questions.

More Buildings in My Neighborhood

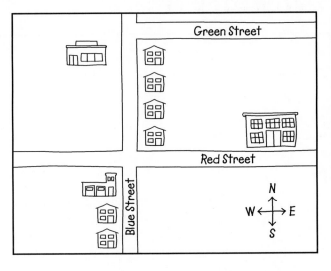

1. What is on the east side of Blue Street?

   a. four schools

   b. four fire halls

   c. four houses

2. Draw three houses south of the school.

3. How would you go from the store to the school?

   _____

   _

   _____

   _

   _____

Geography

Name: _____ **Date:** _____

Directions: Think about your street. Think of symbols. Make a legend. Draw a map of your street.

My Street

N
W ← → E
S

Legend

Name: _____ **Date:** _____

Directions: Look at the map. Cut out the text and glue them on the compass rose. Match the words and symbols on the legend.

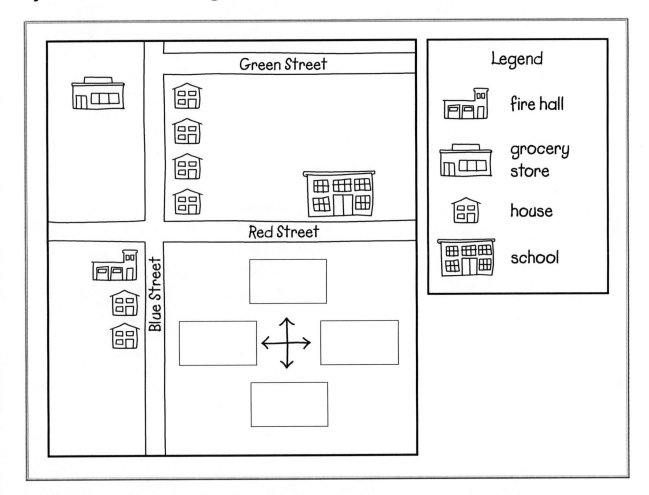

1. Label the compass rose.
   North = N, South = S, East = E, West = W.

2. Add more houses to town.

3. Color the town.

Economics

Name: _____ **Date:** _____

Directions: Look at the pictures. Read the text. Answer the questions.

Doctors and Nurses

People have jobs. Some people help us stay healthy. When we get sick or hurt, we can see a doctor or nurse. Doctors and nurses can help us. They have helping jobs. They help people who are sick or hurt.

1. Based on the text, who helps us if we get sick?

   a. doctor
   b. crossing guard
   c. pilot

2. When do we see a doctor or nurse?
   a. when we want food
   b. when we are sick
   c. when we are excited

51393—180 Days of Social Studies

Name: _____ **Date:** _____

Directions: Look at the pictures. Read the text.
Answer the questions.

Dentists and Hygienists

Some people help us
keep our teeth healthy.
We go to the dentist. The
dentist checks our teeth.

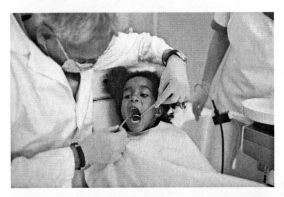

The hygienist helps us
look after our teeth. The
hygienist teaches us
how to brush our teeth.
They have helping jobs.
They help people have
healthy teeth.

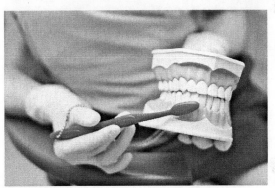

1. Where do you go to have your teeth checked?
   a. fire station
   b. dentist
   c. park

2. Why do we learn to brush our teeth?
   a. to buy a toothbrush
   b. to listen to the hygienist
   c. to take care of our teeth

Economics

Name: _____ **Date:** _____

Directions: Look at the pictures. Answer the questions.

Letter Carriers

1. What are TWO things a letter carrier does?

   a. brings us groceries

   b. brings us packages

   c. brings us letters

2. Draw a picture of something you would like delivered by a letter carrier.

Name: _____ Date: _____

Directions: Look at the picture. Read the text. Answer the questions.

School Helpers

Some people help us learn. We go to school. Our teacher helps us learn new things. The principal helps the teachers. They have helping jobs. They help people learn.

---

1. What is a teacher's job?

   a. to help us learn

   b. to help us clean our teeth

   c. to take us home

2. Teachers and principals are school helpers. What other helpers have jobs at your school?

   _____

   _____

   _____

   _____

   _____

Economics

Name: _____ **Date:** _____

Directions: Look at the pictures. Circle the helping jobs.

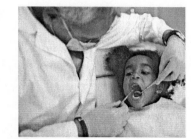

© *Shell Education*

Name: _____ **Date:** _____

Directions: Look at the picture. Read the text. Answer the questions.

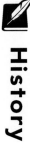

Traveling Long Ago

Long ago, people needed to go places. They did not have cars. They did not have airplanes. They did not go fast. They used horses. They used wagons.

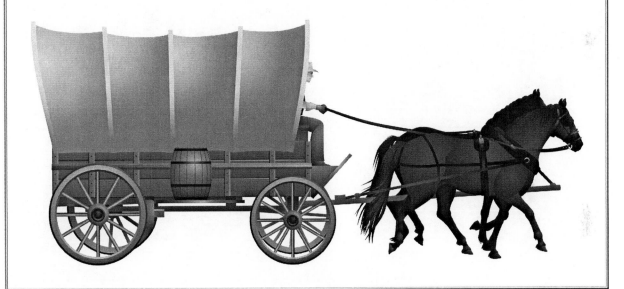

---

1. What did people use to travel long ago?

a. They used cars.

b. They used wagons.

c. They used airplanes.

2. Why did they use horses?

a. to stay at home

b. to feed the horses

c. to go places

© Shell Education

History

Name: _____ **Date:** _____

Directions: Look at the pictures. Answer the questions.

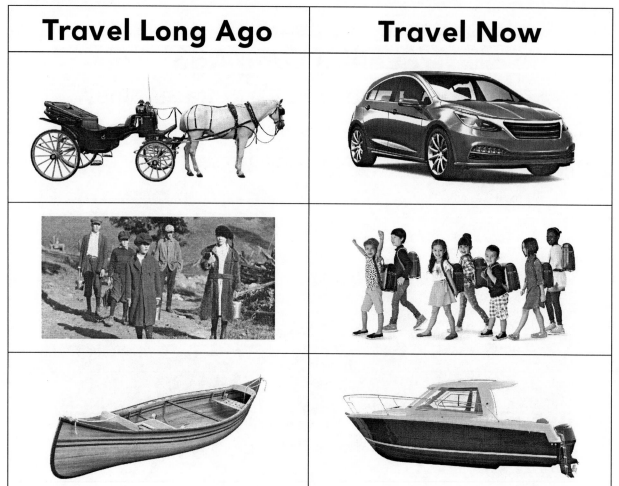

Travel Long Ago	**Travel Now**

1. What is the same?
   a. We fly in planes.
   b. We walk places.
   c. We drive cars.

2. What is NOT the same?
   a. They walked places. We walk places.
   b. They had carriages. We have cars.
   c. They had boats. We have boats.

116

51393—180 Days of Social Studies

© Shell Education

Name: _____ **Date:** _____

Directions: Look at the pictures. Read the text.
Answer the questions.

School Long Ago	School Now
slates to write on	paper and pencils laptops
books	books e-readers
desks	classroom desks and chairs

1. Based on the pictures, what did children have long ago that we don't have?

   a. computer

   b. e-reader

   c. slate

2. Do you want laptops, or do you want slates?

   _____

   _

   _____

History

Name: _____ **Date:** _____

Directions: Look at the picture. Answer the questions.

A Classroom Long Ago

1. What is like your classroom?

_____

_ _

_____

2. What is NOT like your classroom?

_____

_ _

_____

Name: _____ **Date:** _____

Directions: Cut apart the pictures. Glue them in the Venn diagram.

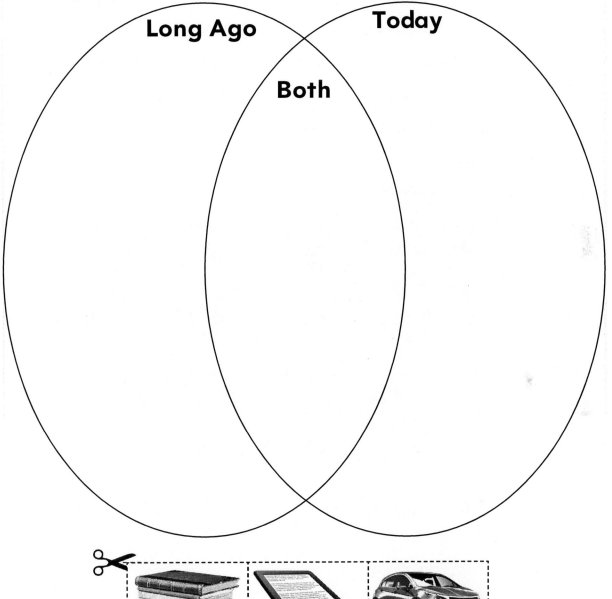

Long Ago   **Today**

Both

Civics

Name: _____ **Date:** _____

Directions: Look at the picture. Read the text. Answer the questions.

Good Citizens Are Good Sports

When we play games, we play fair. We don't cheat. We are good sports. We use kind words. We say, "Good game." We have fun. We are good citizens.

1. If we play fair, we don't _____.

    a. cheat

    b. run

    c. talk

2. Why are they shaking hands in the picture?

    a. They don't like each other.

    b. They say, "Good game."

    c. They say, "What is your name?"

51393—180 Days of Social Studies

© *Shell Education*

Name: _____ **Date:** _____

Directions: Look at the picture. Read the text. Answer the questions.

Good Citizens Respect Other People's Ideas

We listen to our friends. We tell our ideas. They listen to us. We use kind words. If we don't agree, we are still friends.

1. Based on the text, what happens if we don't agree?

   a. We cry.

   b. We are still friends.

   c. We get angry at people.

2. What words do we use to show we respect each other?

   a. We use angry words.

   b. We use hurting words.

   c. We use kind words.

Name: _____ **Date:** _____

Directions: Look at the picture. Answer the questions.

Good Citizens Cooperate

1. What are the children doing?
   a. fighting
   b. drawing
   c. cooperating

2. Draw a picture of you cooperating.

Name: _____ **Date:** _____

Directions: Look at the picture. Read the text. Answer the questions.

Good Citizens Are Honest

We tell the truth. We are honest. We own our actions. We take responsibility.

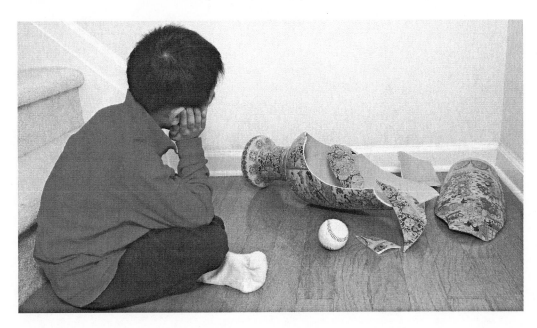

1. What do you think happened?

_____

_ _

_____

2. What would you do if you were this boy?

_____

_ _

_____

Civics

Name: _____ **Date:** _____

Directions: Draw pictures and write about being a good citizen.

```
┌─────────────────────────────────────────────┐
│                                             │
│                                             │
│                                             │
│                                             │
│                                             │
│                                             │
│                                             │
│                                             │
│                                             │
│                                             │
│                                             │
│                                             │
└─────────────────────────────────────────────┘
```

_____

_ _

_____

_ _

_____

_ _

_____

51393—180 Days of Social Studies © *Shell Education*

Name: _____ **Date:** _____

Directions: Look at the picture. Read the text. Answer the questions.

Our World

Here is our world. It has land. It has water. Continents are large pieces of land. Oceans are large bodies of water.

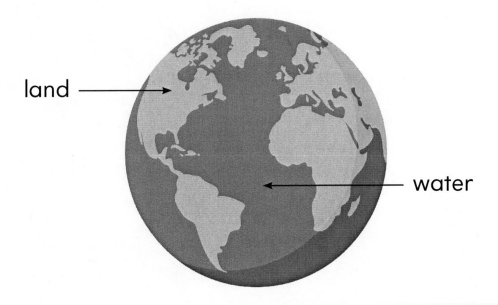

land ———→

water

1. What are continents?

   a. small pieces of land

   b. large pieces of land

   c. large bodies of water

2. What are the large bodies of water around the continents?

   a. rivers

   b. oceans

   c. snow

Geography

Name: _____ **Date:** _____

Directions: Look at the picture. Read the text. Answer the questions.

Mountains and Hills

There are many kinds of land. Mountains are landforms that are very high. Mountains are steep and have peaks. Some mountains were made when the land moved and pushed rocks up. Hills are also high landforms. They are not as high as mountains.

1. What does a mountain look like? Circle TWO answers.
   a. high peaks
   b. lower than a hill
   c. rocky landform

2. What is lowest?
   a. mountain
   b. sky
   c. hill

Name: _____ **Date:** _____

Directions: Look at the pictures. Read the text.
Answer the questions.

Plains, Valleys, and Canyons

A valley is low land. It is
between mountains or hills.

Plains are flat land. They don't
have many trees.

Canyons are deep valleys. The
rock is cut by river water.

---

1. Where is a good place to grow wheat?

   a. mountain

   b. canyon

   c. plain

2. Draw a canyon or valley.

© Shell Education   *51393—180 Days of Social Studies*

Geography

Name: _____ **Date:** _____

Directions: Look at the map. Read the words. Answer the questions.

This is our continent. It is North America. The United States is in North America.

United States

1. Color the United States red. Don't forget Alaska and Hawai'i!

2. Put a blue **X** where you live.

51393—180 Days of Social Studies   © *Shell Education*

Name: _____ **Date:** _____

Directions: Look at the pictures. Use the Word Bank to write the words beside the correct pictures.

Word Bank

plain   mountains   hills   North America

Economics

Name: _____ **Date:** _____

Directions: Look at the pictures. Read the text. Answer the questions.

Bus Drivers

People have jobs. Some people help us go places. Bus drivers help people go to places, such as the store or work. School bus drivers help us go to school and back home. They drive safely. They help us go where we need to go.

1. Where do school bus drivers take us?
   a. to school and back home
   b. to work and back home
   c. to the movies and back home

2. How do bus drivers help us?
   a. They check our teeth.
   b. They take us places safely.
   c. They clean our schools.

Name: _____ **Date:** _____

Directions: Look at the pictures. Read the text.
Answer the questions.

Builders

Some people have building jobs. They build
houses. They build schools. They build stores. They
build places to live and to learn.

---

1. Circle TWO builders above.

2. Based on the text, what are TWO things
builders do?

   a. They build houses.

   b. They build sandcastles.

   c. They build schools.

3. Based on the pictures, what do builders wear?

   a. fancy clothes

   b. top hats

   c. hard hats

Economics

Name: _____ **Date:** _____

Directions: Look at the pictures. Answer the questions.

Firefighters

1. Based on the pictures, what are TWO things firefighters do?

   a. teach us about their jobs and safety

   b. put out fires

   c. build houses

2. Draw a picture of a firefighter working.

Name: _____ **Date:** _____

Directions: Look at the pictures. Read the text.
Answer the questions.

Food Jobs

Some jobs help us get food. Farmers grow food.
Bakers make breads and treats. Cooks make meals.

---

1. Circle TWO people who help us get food.

   a. baker

   b. lifeguard

   c. farmer

2. What food job would you like? Why?

   _____

   _

   _____

   _____

   _____

Name: _____ Date: _____

Economics

Directions: Look at the pictures. Match the helper with the helper's tool.

firefighter

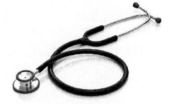

police officer

cook

builder

bus driver

doctor

134

Name: _____ **Date:** _____

Directions: Look at the picture. Read the text. Answer the questions.

Learning from Each Other

Some people lived here a very long time ago. Some people came many years ago. Some came here a few years ago. Many people live here now.

We learn from each other. We learn new ideas. We learn about new foods. We learn new languages. We learn stories. We learn to be friends. We learn from seniors and young people. We learn from teachers.

1. What can we learn from other people in the United States?

    a. new ways to do things

    b. our way to do things

    c. school ways to do things

2. Why can we learn from seniors?

    a. They ask us questions.

    b. They have lived and learned.

    c. They have lesson plans.

History

Name: _____ **Date:** _____

Directions: Look at the picture. Read the text. Answer the questions.

We Learn from American Indians

American Indians teach us.

- Take care of the land.
- Don't take too much from the land.
- Say thank you to the plants and animals.

1. Why should we say thank you to the plants and animals?

   a. The animals give us advice.

   b. The plants like to hear this.

   c. The plants and animals give us food.

2. Why do American Indians take care of the land?

   _____

   _____

   _____

   _____

51393—180 Days of Social Studies

Name: _____ **Date:** _____

Directions: Look at the web diagram. Answer the questions.

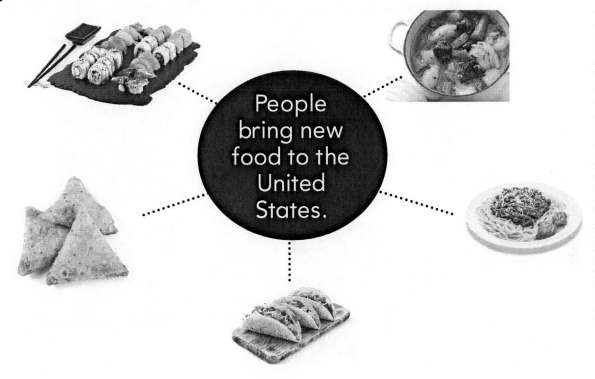

1. Based on the web diagram, what do people bring to the United States?

   a. new houses

   b. new food

   c. new ice rinks

2. What food do you like to eat at home? Why?

   _____

   -

   _____

   -

   _____

History

Name: _____ **Date:** _____

Directions: Look at the pictures. Answer the question.

People Have Traditions	
Christmas 	Kwanzaa 
Chinese New Year 	Diwali 
Hanukkah 	**1.** Draw a tradition you know.

2. Why do we have parties?

_____

- - - - - - - - - - - - - - - - - - -

_____

_____

- - - - - - - - - - - - - - - - - - -

_____

51393—180 Days of Social Studies

Name: _____ **Date:** _____

Directions: Look at the pictures. Read the text.
Answer the question.

> We learn from each other. We learn from our grandparents and other seniors.

1. What can you learn from others?

_____

_____

_____

_____

_____

_____

_____

Civics

Name: _____   **Date:** _____

Directions: Look at the picture. Read the text. Answer the questions.

The American Flag

We have a flag. It is the flag of the United States. It has red and white stripes. It has white stars in a blue field. It is sometimes called "Old Glory." We are proud of our flag.

1. What does our flag look like?

a. red and white stripes and blue stars

b. red and white stripes and white stars

c. blue and white stripes and red stars

2. What is a name for our flag?

a. Old Boy

b. Old Flag

c. Old Glory

Name: _____ **Date:** _____

Directions: Look at the picture. Read the text. Answer the questions.

Our Flag Tells a Story

Today, the United States has 50 states. The flag has 50 stars. There is one star for each state. Long ago, 13 states made the United States. The flag has 13 stripes. There is one stripe for each of the first states.

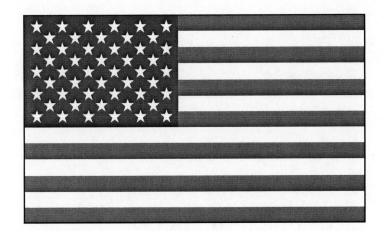

1. What do the stars mean?
   a. The United States has 25 states.
   b. The United States has 50 states.
   c. The states made a new country.

2. What do the stripes mean?
   a. The United States first had 13 states.
   b. We like red and white.
   c. The United States first had 13 cities.

Civics

Name: _____ **Date:** _____

Directions: Look at the pictures. Answer the questions.

The Pledge of Allegiance

I pledge Allegiance to the flag of the United States of America and to the Republic for which it stands, one nation under God, indivisible, with Liberty and Justice for all.

1. What are the children doing?

  a. telling a story to their teacher

  b. waiting for lunch at school

  c. saying the Pledge of Allegiance

2. Draw a picture of you saying the pledge.

51393—180 Days of Social Studies

© *Shell Education*

Name: _____ **Date:** _____

Directions: Look at the pictures. Read the text. Answer the questions.

Civics

Showing Love and Respect

I hug people I love. I use my arms to say I love you. I put my hand on my heart when I say the pledge. This is how I love my country.

1. Why is the girl hugging her mother?

_____

_ _

_____

2. Why do people put their hands on their hearts?

_____

_ _

_____

Name: _____ **Date:** _____

Directions: Look at the picture. Answer the questions.

1. What are the children doing? How do you know?

_____

- -

_____

_____

- -

_____

Name: _____ **Date:** _____

Directions: Look at the pictures. Read the text. Answer the questions.

Climate

Climate is the weather in a place over many years. Some places have cold climates. Some places have hot climates. There are places with dry climates. There are places with wet climates. Some climates have hot seasons and cold seasons. We have many climates in the United States.

1. What is climate?
   a. the weather we have today
   b. the weather over many years
   c. only the weather from yesterday

2. How many climates do we have in the United States?
   a. just one
   b. about three
   c. many

Name: _____ **Date:** _____

Geography

Directions: Look at the pictures. Read the text. Answer the questions.

Clothing

You have cool clothes if you live in a hot climate. You have warm clothes if your climate has a cold season. You may need different clothes in different seasons.

1. Why do you need warm clothes if you live in a cold climate?

   a. to stay cool

   b. to stay wet

   c. to stay warm

2. Why would you need warm clothes and cool clothes?

   a. You like clothes to wear.

   b. Your climate has cold and hot seasons.

   c. Your climate is always hot and never cold.

51393—180 Days of Social Studies

© *Shell Education*

Name: _____ **Date:** _____

Directions: Look at the pictures. Answer the questions.

Shelters

1. Which part of the house protects you from the sun and rain?

   a. driveway

   b. floor

   c. roof

2. Why do houses in hot places need to protect you from the sun?

_____

_____

_____

_____

_____

Geography

Name: _____ **Date:** _____

Directions: Look at pictures. Read the text. Answer the questions.

> We can have fun outside. Some things we do in many climates. Some things don't work in every climate.

1. What can we do outside in most climates?

   a. snow sledding

   b. bike riding

   c. snow skiing

2. What do you like to do outside in your climate?

_____

_____

_____

_____

51393—180 Days of Social Studies

Name: _____ **Date:** _____

Directions: Look at the pictures. Draw a picture that shows the climate where you live. Write about your picture.

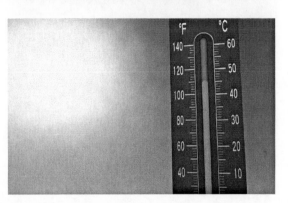

_____

_____

_____

_____

_____

_____

_____

Economics

Name: _____ **Date:** _____

Directions: Look at the pictures. Read the text. Answer the questions.

Goods in the Store

We go to the store. We see goods at the store. We buy goods we need. We might buy goods we want, too.

1. What do we see at the store?

   a. oceans

   b. the moon

   c. goods

2. Based on the pictures and text, what are TWO things we can do in a store?

   a. We look at goods in stores.

   b. We buy goods we need.

   c. We sing about the goods.

Name: _____ **Date:** _____

Directions: Look at the pictures. Read the text. Answer the questions.

Bringing Goods on a Ship

Some goods come from far away. They come on ships. People have jobs on ships. They load the ships. They drive the ships.

---

1. Based on the text, what can goods travel on?

a. scooter   **b.** ship   **c.** tube

2. Which is a job on a ship?
   a. ride on the ship
   b. sleep on the ship
   c. drive the ship

Name: _____ **Date:** _____

Economics

Directions: Look at the picture. Answer the questions.

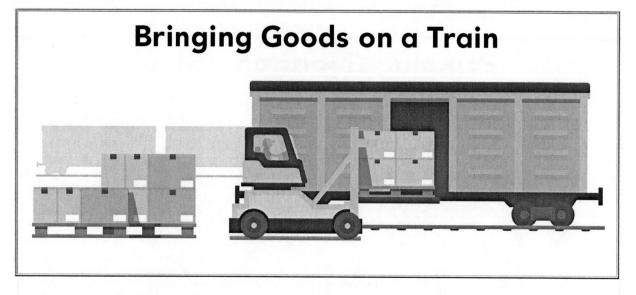

Bringing Goods on a Train

1. Based on the picture, what job does this worker have?

   a. loading and unloading goods

   b. driving the train

   c. sleeping on the train

2. What goods might travel on a train?

_____

- -

_____

- -

_____

- -

_____

51393—180 Days of Social Studies

Name: _____ **Date:** _____

Directions: Look at the pictures. Read the text.
Answer the questions.

Bringing Goods on a Truck

Some people have jobs bringing goods on trucks.
They drive the trucks. They put gas in the trucks.

---

1. How do goods get to a store in a truck?

   a. Someone drives the truck.

   b. The truck slides to the store.

   c. Someone calls the truck.

2. Where have you seen trucks with goods?

   _____

   _____

   _____

   _____

   _____

Economics

Name: _____ **Date:** _____

Directions: How do your jeans get to you? What are the jobs in the process? Draw and label pictures to show the jobs.

First

Next

Then

Last

Name: _____ **Date:** _____

Directions: Look at the picture. Read the text. Answer the questions.

America Celebrates Together

We have holidays. We have fun with our families. We have fun with our friends. We think of our country. We love our country.

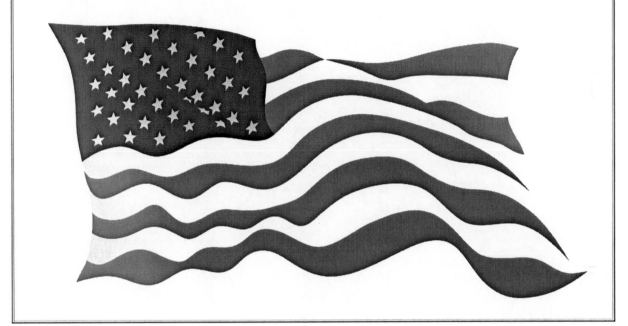

1. Who do we celebrate with?

   a. our computers

   b. our families

   c. our toys

2. What do we think about when we celebrate America?

   a. our video games

   b. our homework

   c. our country

History

Name: _____ **Date:** _____

Directions: Look at the picture. Read the text. Answer the questions.

Thanksgiving Day

Long ago, American Indians helped the Pilgrims. The Pilgrims said thank you. Now some people say thank you on Thanksgiving Day. They eat food. Some of them eat turkey. The see their families.

1. What do people say on Thanksgiving Day?
   a. Let's play.
   b. Thank you.
   c. I am tired.

2. Based on the text and picture, what do some people eat on Thanksgiving Day?
   a. turkey
   b. hot dogs
   c. cereal

51393—180 Days of Social Studies © *Shell Education*

Name: _____ **Date:** _____

Directions: Look at the picture. Answer the questions.

Presidents Day

1. Based on the picture, who do we thank on Presidents Day?

   a. all the principals

   b. all the firefighters

   c. all the presidents

2. Draw a picture for the president. Label it.

Name: _____ **Date:** _____

Directions: Look at the pictures. Read the text. Answer the questions.

Independence Day

Independence Day is on the Fourth of July. It is the country's birthday.

Fourth of July in Our Town

8:00 a.m.	pancake breakfast
10:00 a.m.	parade
12:00 noon	picnic
2:00 p.m.	games and rides
6:00 p.m.	BBQ
9:00 p.m.	fireworks

1. What TWO Fourth of July things are we doing?

   a. fireworks

   b. picnic

   c. nap

2. What do you like to do on the Fourth of July? Draw a picture, and label it.

History

Name: _____ **Date:** _____

Directions: Look at the diagram. Read the text. Write a letter.

We live in the United States.

We say thank you to the presidents.

We say thank you for our country.

We celebrate.

We say thank you for food.

1. Get a piece of paper. Write a letter to the president. Tell what you celebrate. Tell why you say thank you.

Civics

Name: _____ **Date:** _____

Directions: Look at the picture. Read the text. Answer the questions.

Mount Rushmore

There is a special mountain in the United States. It is called Mount Rushmore. It shows the heads of four presidents. The heads are very big. These men helped our country. These men loved the United States. We think about the presidents. We learn how they helped our country.

1. How many heads are on Mount Rushmore?
   a. three heads
   b. four heads
   c. five heads

2. Why are these heads on the mountain?
   a. They lived on the mountain.
   b. They went to the mountain.
   c. They were presidents.

Name: _____ **Date:** _____

Directions: Look at the picture. Read the text. Answer the questions.

The Liberty Bell

The Liberty Bell is very old. It was rung long ago. It tells us that we must plan good laws. It tells us that women and men are free. *Liberty* means freedom. The bell tells us to spread freedom.

1. What does the Liberty Bell tell us?
   a. It tells us it is time for school.
   b. It tells us that everyone is free.
   c. It tell us that we are late.

2. Based on the text, what should we spread?
   a. fear
   b. cheerfulness
   c. freedom

Name: _____ Date: _____

Directions: Look at the picture. Answer the questions.

Civics

The Martin Luther King Jr. Memorial

Dr. King asked people to be fair and to get along.

1. What did Dr. King want?

   a. for people to fight each other

   b. for people to wait for him

   c. for people to to be fair

2. What can you do to be fair to other people?

_____

_ _

_____

_ _

_____

51393—180 Days of Social Studies

© *Shell Education*

Name: _____ **Date:** _____

Directions: Look at the pictures. Read the text. Answer the questions.

Civics

Symbols

We have symbols of our families. We love our families. We have symbols of our country. We are proud of our country.

1. How do we feel about our country?

   a. sad

   b. proud

   c. lost

2. What is a symbol for your family?

_____

_____

_____

Name: _____ Date: _____

Directions: Look at the pictures. Circle landmarks of the United States. Make a new symbol that shows something special about our country. Give it a title.

Civics

© Shell Education

Name: _____ **Date:** _____

Directions: Look at the picture. Read the text. Answer the questions.

Where We Live

An environment is the plants and animals around you. It is the water and land, too. People live in different places. Some people live near water. Some people live on mountains. Other people live in deserts. Some people are in hot places. Some people are in cool places. Different things grow in these places.

1. Circle TWO things that the text says are in an environment.

   a. water

   b. plants

   c. moons

2. Circle TWO environments where people live.

   a. mountain

   b. moon

   c. desert

Geography

Name: _____ **Date:** _____

Directions: Look at the pictures. Read the text. Answer the questions.

People build places to live. They build in many environments.

1

2

1. Which place gets more rain?
   a. picture 1
   b. picture 2
   c. both pictures

2. What types of plants are in picture 1?
   a. ocean plants
   b. desert plants
   c. corn plants

Name: _____ **Date:** _____

Directions: Look at the picture. Answer the questions.

1. What words describe this environment?

   a. hot and dry

   b. cold and rainy

   c. muddy and wet

2. What is the same as where you live? What is different?

_____

_ _

_____

_ _

_____

Name: _____ **Date:** _____

Directions: Look at the picture. Answer the questions.

1. What words describe this environment?

   a. grassy and flat plain

   b. rocky and mountains

   c. snowy and rolling hills

2. Describe your environment.

_____

_____

_____

_____

_____

Name: _____ **Date:** _____

Directions: Look at the pictures. Match the clothes to the places.

Name: _____ Date: _____

Economics

Directions: Look at the pictures. Read the text. Answer the questions.

Jobs in the Grocery Store

We buy food at the grocery store. People work in the grocery store. They have jobs. Some people unload goods from the trucks. Some people put goods on the shelves. Cashiers take money for goods. Some people clean the store.

1. Why do we go to the grocery store?
   a. We buy cars.
   b. We buy food.
   c. We buy hammers.

2. Circle TWO jobs in a grocery store.
   a. cashier
   b. cleaner
   c. teacher

Name: _____ **Date:** _____

Directions: Look at the picture. Read the text. Answer the questions.

Why We Have Jobs

People have jobs. There are many jobs. People work hard. Most people work to get money.

1. Why do most people work?

   a. to be healthy

   b. to get money

   c. to climb stairs

2. Based on the text, how do people work?

   a. loudly

   b. softly

   c. hard

Economics

Name: _____ **Date:** _____

Directions: Look at the pictures. Answer the questions.

Why We Earn Money

1. Based on the pictures, why do people earn money?
   a. to hold it
   b. to work
   c. to buy food

2. What would you buy if you earned some money?

_____

_____

_____

_____

_____

_____

_____

Name: _____ **Date:** _____

Directions: Look at the pictures. Read the text. Answer the questions.

Being Paid

People do their jobs. They get paid money when they work. People can get bills and coins. People can get a paycheck. Money can be in a wallet. Money can be in a purse. Money can be in the bank.

1. Circle TWO places where the author says you can put money.

   a. in the bank

   b. in a wallet

   c. under your desk

2. Where would you keep your money when you go shopping? Draw a picture, and label it.

Name: _____ **Date:** _____

Economics

Directions: Look at your paycheck. Write your name. You can spend your paycheck. Circle things you want or need to buy.

Paycheck for _____

Ten dollars $10

$1

$2

$2

$2

$1

$2

$1

$1

$2

$2

Name: _____ **Date:** _____

Directions: Look at the picture. Read the text. Answer the questions.

People Who Help

We have special days. We think about people who help. We say thank you to helpers. We say thank to helpers who died.

---

1. Based on the text, who do we say thank you to on special days?

   a. children

   b. pets

   c. helpers

2. Based on the text, why do we have special days?

   a. to think about people who help

   b. to think about our school

   c. to think about our friends

Name: _____ **Date:** _____

Directions: Look at the picture. Read the text. Answer the questions.

Martin Luther King Jr. Day

We think about Martin Luther King Jr. He said we need to be fair. His day is in January. We think about being fair. We think about being kind. We try to get along with each other.

I HAVE A DREAM

1. When is Martin Luther King Jr. Day?
   a. in August
   b. in July
   c. in January

2. What did King say?
   a. We need to be angry.
   b. We need to be fair.
   c. We need to be smart.

Name: _____ **Date:** _____

Directions: Look at the picture. Answer the questions.

Memorial Day

1. What do we put on the graves on Memorial Day?

   a. soap

   b. food

   c. flags

2. What would you say to these people if you could talk to them? Tell them how you feel.

   _____

   _____

   _____

   _____

   _____

Name: _____ **Date:** _____

Directions: Look at the pictures. Read the text. Answer the questions.

History

Veterans Day

Veterans served the United States. They helped us. We say thank you for their help.

---

1. Why do we thank veterans?

   a. They say please.

   b. They are nice people.

   c. They helped the United States.

2. Write a sentence to say thank you to a veteran.

_____

- -

_____

_____

- -

_____

Name: _____ **Date:** _____

Directions: Look at the pictures. Draw a picture, and label it.

_____

_ _

_____

Civics

Name: _____ **Date:** _____

Directions: Look at the picture. Read the text. Answer the questions.

Being a Good Citizen

We live in the United States. We are good citizens. We make good decisions. We talk about ideas. We vote to decide things. We help others. We take care of our country. We get along. We are fair.

1. Based on the text, what do good citizens do?

   a. argue with each other

   b. help each other

   c. talk too much

2. Where do you live?

   a. in Africa

   b. in Uruguay

   c. in the United States

Name: _____ **Date:** _____

Directions: Read the text. Answer the questions.

Deciding Together

In the United States, people can vote to decide things. Good citizens vote. In my class, we talk about what we want. Then, we vote. We are good citizens in my class. Today, we had a vote about a party. We picked the party.

Popcorn Party	Ice Cream Party
卌 I	卌 卌 II

1. Which party did we pick?
   a. popcorn party
   b. ice cream party
   c. no party

2. Why did we vote?
   a. to pick the party most people want
   b. to stop the party from taking place
   c. to pick a hot dog party

Civics

Name: _____ **Date:** _____

Directions: Look at the pictures. Answer the questions.

Helping Others

1. How are these children being good citizens?

_____

_ _

_____

2. How do you help other people?

_____

_ _

_____

51393—180 Days of Social Studies

Name: _____ **Date:** _____

Directions: Look at the pictures. Read the text.
Answer the questions.

Cooperating

We get along with each other. We cooperate. We
are fair. We share.

1. Are these people cooperating? Tell how.

_____

_ _ _ _ _ _ _ _ _ _ _ _ _ _ _ _ _

_____

_____

_ _ _ _ _ _ _ _ _ _ _ _ _ _ _ _ _

_____

2. What is one way you cooperate?

_____

_ _ _ _ _ _ _ _ _ _ _ _ _ _ _ _ _

_____

Name: _____ **Date:** _____

Directions: Write words or draw pictures to finish the web.

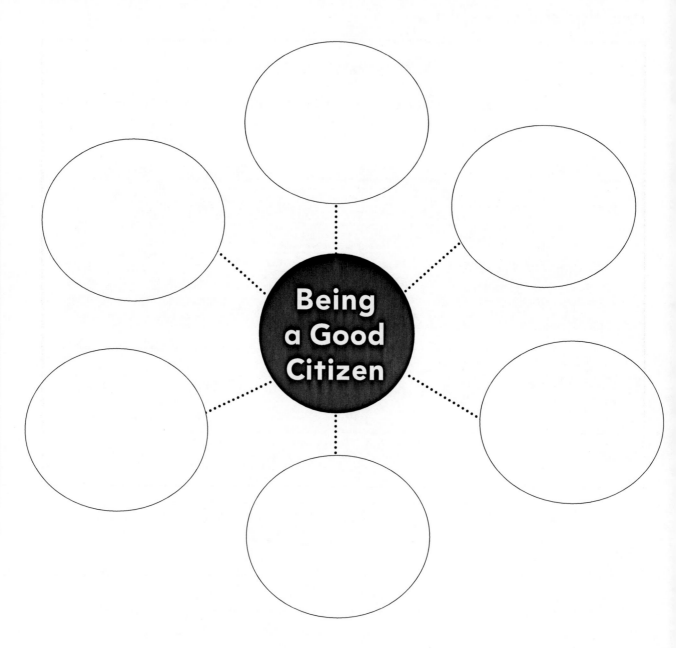

Being a Good Citizen

Word Bank

sharing	yelling	fighting
cooperating	taking care	voting
being selfish	being fair	being kind

51393—180 Days of Social Studies

Civics

Name: _____ **Date:** _____

Directions: Look at the picture. Read the text. Answer the questions.

Changing the Environment

People live in many environments. Sometimes, we change the environment. We change it so we can do things we want. We heat our houses. We have lights at night. We build roads. We build dams. This picture shows a mall. They made a ski hill inside!

1. In what TWO ways do we change our environment?

 a. We use lights at night.

 b. We sing songs.

 c. We heat our homes.

2. What is in the mall?

 a. mountain lions

 b. a ski hill

 c. a space ship

Geography

Name: _____ **Date:** _____

Directions: Look at the picture. Read the text. Answer the questions.

Greenhouses

People make greenhouses. They can grow plants when it is cold. They can grow plants when it is dry. They can grow plants without soil.

1. What are greenhouses used for?

   a. to grow puppies

   b. to grow plants

   c. to make things cold

2. How can a greenhouse change the environment?

   a. It can be warmer.

   b. It can be rockier.

   c. It can be louder.

51393—180 Days of Social Studies   © *Shell Education*

Name: _____ Date: _____

Directions: Look at the pictures. Answer the questions.

People Build Dams

1. What is one thing a dam can make?

   a. food

   b. lakes

   c. highways

2. Describe the dams. What do you think they are for?

_____

- -

_____

_____

- -

_____

_____

- -

_____

Geography

Name: _____ **Date:** _____

Directions: Look at the pictures. Read the text. Answer the questions.

People Build Places for Sports

People change the environment to have fun. We can skate when it is hot. We can swim when it is cold.

 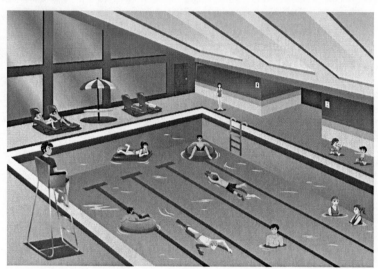

1. Why do we do sports inside?
   a. It is not too hot or too cold.
   b. We can rest or sleep.
   c. It is not too noisy.

2. How do you have fun inside?

_____

_ _ _ _ _ _ _ _ _ _ _ _ _ _ _ _ _ _

_____

Name: _____ **Date:** _____

Directions: Look at the pictures. Circle the pictures where people have changed the environment.

Economics

Name: _____ **Date:** _____

Directions: Look at the picture. Read the text. Answer the questions.

Jobs in My Classroom

We all have jobs in my classroom. We all help. We keep the classroom safe and clean. We help our teacher. My teacher gives us classroom money.

1. Who has a job in the classroom?
   a. We all have jobs.
   b. Three people have jobs.
   c. Only the girls have jobs.

2. Why do we have jobs at school?
   a. We help our mothers.
   b. We help the teacher.
   c. We help our brothers.

Name: _____ **Date:** _____

Directions: Look at the pictures. Read the text. Answer the questions.

Our Jobs

I am the line leader. I walk at the front of the line. I earn one classroom dollar.

I check the coats and shoes. I make sure no one trips on a shoe. I pick up coats. I earn one classroom dollar.

---

1. Why does she earn one classroom dollar?

　a. She listens to her friends.

　b. She talks to her friends.

　c. She is the line leader.

2. Why does he check the coats and shoes?

　a. to see the colors

　b. to make sure no one trips on a shoe

　c. to go to the coat rack and get a coat

Name: _____ Date: _____

Directions: Look at the pictures. Read the text. Answer the questions.

Economics

More Jobs

I hand out paper and books. I help the teacher. I earn one classroom dollar.

I am the door holder. I hold the door open when we come into the school. No one gets hurt by the door. I earn one classroom dollar.

---

1. What is one job in this classroom?

　a. singing songs for everyone

　b. handing out snacks for everyone

　c. handing out paper and books

2. Why do we hold the door for other people?

_____

_ _ _ _ _ _ _ _ _ _ _ _ _ _ _ _ _

_____

Name: _____ **Date:** _____

Directions: Look at the pictures. Read the text. Answer the questions.

We Help in Our Classroom

We have classroom jobs. We help each other. We work hard. We earn classroom dollars when we do our jobs.

 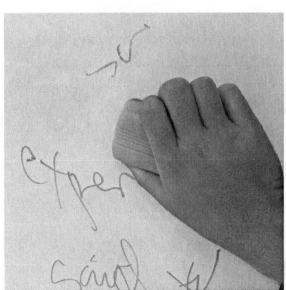

1. What do we earn when we do our jobs?

a. real money

b. books and paper

c. classroom dollars

2. What are some jobs in your classroom?

_____

_ _

_____

Economics

Name: _____ **Date:** _____

Directions: Here is our classroom store. You earned five classroom dollars. What would you buy? Why?

$2

$1

$1

$1

$2

$3

_____

_____

_____

_____

_____

_____

_____

194

ANSWER KEY

Week 1—History

Day 1
1. b
2. c

Day 2
1. c
2. b

Day 3
1. b
2. Drawings will vary.

Day 4
1. b
2. Drawings will vary.

Day 5
Drawings will vary.

Week 2—Civics

Day 1
1. b
2. a

Day 2
1. c
2. b

Day 3
1. b
2. Responses will vary.

Day 4
1. c
2. Drawings will vary.

Day 5
Circle all pictures except the two angry girls.

Week 3—Geography

Day 1
1. b
2. a

Day 2
1. c
2. a

Day 3
1. b
2. Responses may vary. On the rug or at their desks would be valid responses.

Day 4
1. Circle desks and table. Allow for computer.
2. Responses will vary.

Day 5
Circle picture on the left.
Labels: teacher's desk or desk, blackboard or board, desks or students' desks

Week 4—Economics

Day 1
1. a; b
2. b

Day 2
1. c
2. a

Day 3
Drawings and responses will vary.

Day 4
Needs: to be safe from the storm; shelter (house)
Wants: dry clothes; a hug
Other responses will vary.

Day 5
Drawing of a purple jacket; drawing of a healthy drink (e.g., water)
Filled-in words: soda or soft drink; home or house; castle

ANSWER KEY *(cont.)*

Week 5—History

Day 1
1. b
2. a

Day 2
1. c
2. b

Day 3
1. a
2. Responses and drawings will vary. Could include happy, content, or relieved.

Day 4
1. b
2. They both have stars and stripes. One flag has more stars than the other flag.

Day 5
Francis Scott Key; Harriet Tubman; Squanto

Week 6—Civics

Day 1
1. b
2. c

Day 2
1. a
2. b

Day 3
1. c
2. Drawings will vary.

Day 4
1. c
2. Responses will vary.

Day 5
Pictures should match labels.

Week 7—Geography

Day 1
1. b
2. b

Day 2
1. c
2. a

Day 3
1. c
2. b

Day 4
1. Drawing of a tree in upper left and lower right corners of map; bush in upper right corner of map; bush symbol and tree symbol on legend
2. Drawings will vary.

Day 5
Appropriate symbols should be drawn in legend.

Week 8—Economics

Day 1
1. a; b
2. a; c

Day 2
1. b
2. a; c

Day 3
Students may mark the following: clock; bulletin board; board; ruler; brush; pointer; desks; chairs; books; backpack; and clothing.
1. Responses will vary.
2. Responses will vary.

Day 4
Drawings will vary.

Day 5
Drawings should include toy truck, bags, carrots, lettuce, bread, eggs, cookies, apples, milk, and table.

196

51393—180 Days of Social Studies

ANSWER KEY *(cont.)*

Week 9—History

Day 1
1. c
2. a

Day 2
1. b
2. a
3. Drawings will vary.

Day 3
1. b
2. Responses will vary.

Day 4
1. b
2. Drawings will vary.

Day 5
Martin Luther King Jr.; Neil Armstrong; Mae C. Jemison; Thomas Edison

Week 10—Civics

Day 1
1. b
2. a
3. Drawings will vary.

Day 2
1. c
2. b

Day 3
1. a
2. Responses will vary.

Day 4
1. Responses will vary.
2. Responses will vary.

Day 5
Matching: 1 and 3; 2 and 4; 3 and 1; 4 and 5; 5 and 2

Week 11—Geography

Day 1
1. c
2. b

Day 2
1. b
2. a; b

Day 3
1. Fences are colored blue.
2. Flower symbols are applied.
3. a
4. Trees are drawn near houses.

Day 4
1. Drawings will vary.
2. Drawings will vary.

Day 5
Drawings of symbols for fire hall, post office, store, tree

Week 12—Economics

Day 1
1. a; c
2. All three of the answers are correct.

Day 2
1. b; c
2. a; b

Day 3
Goods in red: chocolate chip cookies; apple
Services in blue: clean up; pick up trash; wipe off boards; sharpen pencils
1. Responses will vary.
2. Responses will vary.

Day 4
Responses will vary. All of Will's tasks should be included on the Venn diagram.

Day 5
Goods: football; carrot; book; shoes
Services: painter; doctor; firefighter; bulldozer operator

ANSWER KEY *(cont.)*

Week 13—History

Day 1
1. a
2. b

Day 2
1. a
2. b

Day 3
1. b
2. Drawings will vary.
3. Responses will vary.

Day 4
1. c
2. Drawings will vary.

Day 5
Same: fried egg; cat; dog
Different: log cabin; cauldron over fire; airplane; longhouse; woman in pioneer clothes

Week 14—Civics

Day 1
1. b
2. a
3. a; c

Day 2
1. c
2. c

Day 3
1. c
2. Responses will vary.

Day 4
1. Responses will vary.
2. Responses will vary.

Day 5
Responses will vary but should include concepts of safety and respect.

Week 15—Geography

Day 1
1. c
2. Door should be added to legend.
3. b

Day 2
1. b
2. b

Day 3
Drawings will vary but all images in the legend should be included on the map.

Day 4
Drawings will vary but all images in the legend should be included on the map.

Day 5
Drawings will vary.

Week 16—Economics

Day 1
1. b
2. b

Day 2
1. b
2. c

Day 3
1. c
2. Responses will vary but should include scissors or razor and chair; may include brush, comb, apron, shampoo.

Day 4
1. Drawings and responses will vary.
2. Drawings and responses will vary.

Day 5
Producer mistakes: swimmer; skateboarder

ANSWER KEY *(cont.)*

Week 17—History

Day 1
1. b
2. b

Day 2
1. a
2. b

Day 3
1. Responses will vary but could include teacher and children.
2. Responses will vary but could include what they are doing and clothing.

Day 4
1. c
2. Responses will vary.

Day 5
1. Drawings and responses will vary.

Week 18—Civics

Day 1
1. c
2. a

Day 2
1. c
2. b

Day 3
1. a
2. Responses will vary.

Day 4
1. Responses will vary.
2. Responses will vary.

Day 5
Circle: doctor; bus driver; teacher; crossing guard; police officer
1. Responses will vary.

Week 19—Geography

Day 1
1. b
2. c

Day 2
1. c
2. a

Day 3
1. c
2. Three houses are drawn south of the school on Red Street.
3. Walk south on Blue Street; turn east on Red Street to the school.

Day 4
Drawings will vary.

Day 5
1. Students should label the compass rose.
2. Drawings will vary.
3. Drawings will vary.

Week 20—Economics

Day 1
1. a
2. b

Day 2
1. b
2. c

Day 3
1. b; c
2. Drawings will vary.

Day 4
1. a
2. Responses will vary.

Day 5
Circle: doctor; dentist; teacher; police officer; pilot; firefighter; crossing guard

ANSWER KEY *(cont.)*

Week 21—History

Day 1
1. b
2. c

Day 2
1. b
2. b

Day 3
1. c
2. Responses will vary.

Day 4
1. Responses will vary but could include window, bulletin board, and bookshelf.
2. Responses will vary but could include desks, floor, and wood stove.

Day 5
Long ago: slate; horse and buggy
Today: car; airplane; computer; notebook and pencil
Middle: canoe; books
Allow for possible responses: notebook could be in the middle; horse and buggy could be in the middle.

Week 22—Civics

Day 1
1. a
2. b

Day 2
1. b
2. c

Day 3
1. c
2. Drawings will vary.

Day 4
1. The boy broke the vase with the ball.
2. Responses will vary but could include tell the truth, clean it up, and say sorry.

Day 5
Drawings and responses will vary.

Week 23—Geography

Day 1
1. b
2. b

Day 2
1. a; c
2. c

Day 3
1. c
2. Drawings will vary.

Day 4
1. The United States (including possibly Alaska and Hawaii) are colored red.
2. Responses will vary.
3. The map is labeled North America.

Day 5
Mountains; North America; plain; hills

Week 24—Economics

Day 1
1. a
2. b

Day 2
1. Circle roofer and bricklayer.
2. a; c
3. c

Day 3
1. a; b
2. Drawings will vary.

Day 4
1. a; c
2. Responses will vary.

Day 5
Matching: 1 and 4; 2 and 5; 3 and 6; 4 and 3; 5 and 2; 6 and 1

ANSWER KEY *(cont.)*

Week 25—History

Day 1
1. a
2. b

Day 2
1. c
2. Responses will vary but could include they want the land to stay healthy.

Day 3
1. b
2. Responses will vary.

Day 4
Drawings and responses will vary.

Day 5
Responses will vary.

Week 26—Civics

Day 1
1. b
2. c

Day 2
1. b
2. a

Day 3
1. c
2. Drawings will vary.

Day 4
1. She loves her mother.
2. They show love and/or respect for their country.

Day 5
1. They are pledging allegiance. The evidence for this statement will vary.

Week 27—Geography

Day 1
1. b
2. c

Day 2
1. c
2. b

Day 3
1. c
2. Responses will vary but could include the sun can burn; you could get too hot.

Day 4
1. b
2. Responses will vary.

Day 5
Responses and drawings will vary.

Week 28—Economics

Day 1
1. c
2. a; b

Day 2
1. b
2. c

Day 3
1. a
2. Responses will vary.

Day 4
1. a
2. Responses will vary.

Day 5
Responses will vary but could include someone making the jeans; someone transporting the jeans on a boat/truck; someone putting the jeans in the store; someone selling the jeans to the buyer.

ANSWER KEY *(cont.)*

Week 29—History

Day 1
1. b
2. c

Day 2
1. b
2. a

Day 3
1. c
2. Drawings and responses will vary.

Day 4
1. a; b
2. Drawings and responses will vary.

Day 5
Responses will vary.

Week 30—Civics

Day 1
1. b
2. c

Day 2
1. b
2. c

Day 3
1. c
2. Responses will vary.

Day 4
1. b
2. Responses will vary.

Day 5
Circle: Martin Luther King Jr. Memorial;
Mount Rushmore; Liberty Bell
Drawings and responses will vary.

Week 31—Geography

Day 1
1. a; b
2. a; c

Day 2
1. b
2. b

Day 3
1. a
2. Responses will vary.

Day 4
1. b
2. Responses will vary.

Day 5
Matching: 1 and 4; 2 and 3; 3 and 2; 4 and 1

Week 32—Economics

Day 1
1. b
2. a; b

Day 2
1. b
2. c

Day 3
1. c
2. Responses will vary.

Day 4
1. a; b
2. Drawings and responses will vary.

Day 5
Responses will vary but total should be $10 or less.

ANSWER KEY *(cont.)*

Week 33—History

Day 1
1. c
2. a

Day 2
1. c
2. b

Day 3
1. c
2. Responses will vary.

Day 4
1. c
2. Responses will vary.

Day 5
Drawings and responses will vary.

Week 34—Civics

Day 1
1. b
2. c

Day 2
1. b
2. a

Day 3
1. They are helping others.
2. Responses will vary.

Day 4
1. Responses will vary.
2. Responses will vary.

Day 5
Drawings will vary. Words from Word Bank could include sharing; cooperating; taking care; being fair; voting; being kind.

Week 35—Geography

Day 1
1. a; c
2. b

Day 2
1. b
2. a

Day 3
1. b
2. Responses will vary but could include making power and/or making a lake.

Day 4
1. a
2. Responses will vary.

Day 5
Circle: highway, dam, houses, greenhouse

Week 36—Economics

Day 1
1. a
2. b

Day 2
1. c
2. b

Day 3
1. c
2. Reponses will vary but could include so no one gets hurt; to be safe; to be polite.

Day 4
1. c
2. Responses will vary.

Day 5
Responses will vary but total should be $5 or less.

Response Rubric

Teacher Directions: The answer key provides answers for the multiple-choice and short-answer questions. This rubric can be used for any open-ended questions where student responses vary. Evaluate student work to determine how many points out of 12 students earn.

Student Name: _____

	4 Points	3 Points	2 Points	1 Point
Content Knowledge	Gives right answers. Answers are based on text and prior knowledge.	Gives right answers based on text.	Gives mostly right answers based on text.	Gives incorrect answers.
Analysis	Thinks about the content, and draws strong inferences/conclusions.	Thinks about the content, and draws mostly correct inferences/conclusions.	Thinks about the content, and draws somewhat correct inferences/conclusions.	Thinks about the content, and draws incorrect inferences/conclusions.
Explanation	Explains and supports answers fully.	Explains and supports answers with some evidence.	Explains and supports answers with little evidence.	Provides no support for answers.

Total: _____

Practice Page Item Analysis

Teacher Directions: Record how many multiple-choice questions students answered correctly. Then, record their rubric totals for Day 5. Total the four weeks of scores, and record that number in the Overall column.

Circle Week Range: 1–4 5–8 9–12 13–16 17–20 21–24 25–28 29–32 33–36						
Student Name	**Day 1** Text Analysis	**Day 2** Text Analysis	**Day 3** Primary Source or Visual Text	**Day 4** Making Connections	**Day 5** Synthesis and Application	**Overall**
Ryan	2, 2, 2, 2	2, 2, 2, 2	2, 2, 2, 1	2, 2, 2, 1	12, 9, 11, 12	74

Student Item Analysis By Discipline

Teacher Directions: Record how many multiple-choice questions students answered correctly. Then, record their rubric totals for Day 5. Total the four weeks of scores, and record that number in the Overall column.

Student Name:						
History Weeks	**Day 1** Text Analysis	**Day 2** Text Analysis	**Day 3** Primary Source or Visual Text	**Day 4** Making Connections	**Day 5** Synthesis and Application	**Overall**
1						
5						
9						
13						
17						
21						
25						
29						
33						
Civics Weeks	**Day 1** Text Analysis	**Day 2** Text Analysis	**Day 3** Primary Source or Visual Text	**Day 4** Making Connections	**Day 5** Synthesis and Application	**Overall**
2						
6						
10						
14						
18						
22						
26						
30						
34						

Student Item Analysis By Discipline *(cont.)*

Student Name:

Geography Weeks	**Day 1** Text Analysis	**Day 2** Text Analysis	**Day 3** Primary Source or Visual Text	**Day 4** Making Connections	**Day 5** Synthesis and Application	**Overall**
3						
7						
11						
15						
19						
23						
27						
31						
35						

Economics Weeks	**Day 1** Text Analysis	**Day 2** Text Analysis	**Day 3** Primary Source or Visual Text	**Day 4** Making Connections	**Day 5** Synthesis and Application	**Overall**
4						
8						
12						
16						
20						
24						
28						
32						
36						

Digital Resources

To access the digital resources, go to this website and enter the following code: 24293213.
www.teachercreatedmaterials.com/administrators/download-files/

Rubric and Analysis Sheets

Resource	Filename
Response Rubric	responserubric.pdf
Practice Page Item Analysis	itemanalysis.pdf
	itemanalysis.docx
	itemanalysis.xlsx
Student Item Analysis by Discipline	socialstudiesanalysis.pdf
	socialstudiesanalysis.docx
	socialstudiesanalysis.xlsx

Standards and Themes

Resource	Filename
Weekly Topics and Themes	topicsthemes.pdf
Standards Charts	standards.pdf